GAME
PLANS
FOR
SUCCESS

Winning Strategies
for Business and Life
from Ten Top
NFL Head Coaches

Edited by **Ray Didinger**

With a Foreword by **Barry Sheehy**

LITTLE, BROWN AND COMPANY
Boston   New York   Toronto   London

PHOTO CREDITS

Marty Schottenheimer: Paul Jasienski/NFL Photos
Joe Gibbs: Scott Cunningham/NFL Photos
Mike Ditka: Brian Spurlock/NFL Photos
Dennis Green: David Drapkin/NFL Photos
Tom Coughlin: Gerry Gallegos/NFL Photos
Bud Grant: Billy Robin McFarland/NFL Photos
Norv Turner: Paul Spinelli/NFLP
Bill Walsh: Michael Zagaris/NFL Photos
George Seifert: Dave Stock/NFL Photos
Chuck Noll: George Gojkovich/NFL Photos

First Edition

Library of Congress Cataloging-in-Publication Data

Game plans for success : winning strategies for business and life from
    ten top NFL head coaches / edited by Ray Didinger ; with a foreword
    by Barry Sheehy. — 1st ed.
        p.   cm.
    ISBN 0-316-59189-0
    1. Football — Coaching — Philosophy. 2. Success. 3. Management.
    4. Success in business. I. Didinger, Ray.
    GV954.4.G36   1995
    796.322'07'7 — dc20   95-16265

10 9 8 7 6 5 4 3 2 1

MV-NY

Published simultaneously in Canada by Little, Brown & Company (Canada) Limited

Printed in the United States of America

Contents

Foreword

by Barry Sheehy

Few sports have been as successful as pro football in producing great teams and extraordinary leaders to guide them. In *Game Plans for Success,* you will read about the management philosophies and leadership techniques of a select group of men — NFL head coaches — who are involved in the unique mix of sports, business, and entertainment that is the National Football League.

This is a first-person chronicle written by men who have recognized the enormous power of a holistic approach to performance. Not only have these coaches discovered and embraced the principles of a basic value system and its power to generate and regenerate success, they also have learned to work under enormous pressure and to win at a world-class level. And, outward appearances to the contrary, they are people who are dealing in a corporate environment that is every bit as complex and demanding as the manufacture of automobiles or silicon chips.

It is no accident that successful teams are characterized not only by superb on-field performance but also by top-notch off-field management. No organization gets to the Super Bowl only because it has a talented football team. Poor performance in the front office sooner or later seeps into the product on the field. A successful NFL franchise is a winning organization that, as any successful business, must perform well in every facet of the operation.

The NFL game is so exciting to watch that it is easy for us to forget how much of a business it is. We tend to think of "real" businesses as having an association with bricks, mortar, plants, and equipment. Such a traditional view is outdated — a quick look at today's economic landscape explodes this industrial-age business model. Tourism, not chemicals or steel, is now the world's largest industry. Health care, not heavy industry, is the largest, fastest-growing segment of our national economy. And entertainment (including professional sports), which is increasingly inseparable from telecommunications, employs more people than automobile manufacturing and mining combined.

Thus, the NFL fits the paradigm of a twenty-first-century enterprise better than most corporations in today's economy. Think about it. The NFL adds value not by making things but by providing a service (i.e., entertainment). This offering cannot be inventoried except electronically. The only permanent bricks and mortar required to run this multibillion-dollar enterprise are stadiums and training complexes; the true medium of distribution is digital. The enterprise works because it is decentralized and operates close to its customers in the form of local team franchises. In fact, the NFL turns its customers into fans, an accomplishment every business in America would like to emulate. And, while it has developed its game, the NFL also has built itself into a brand of immense power. The NFL logo means something to consumers. It is an intangible asset of exceptional value.

We need new models, new structures, and new ideas to cope with the challenges of a new economy. In this context, the NFL — the most successful of sports leagues — provides an important and innovative model.

One of the things that makes the NFL so interesting is that it acts, in many ways, like a "virtual corporation." Players, process is becoming increasingly important to business. As product lifestyles shrink, so do the life cycles of most businesses, making the same kind of regeneration NFL teams deal with annually one of the greatest challenges facing business today.

Corporations that are unable to renew themselves perish quickly. In fact, the capacity to master change and renewal may be the most important of all corporate competencies, and there are no better examples of this competency in action than those found in this book.

In the course of reading *Game Plans for Success,* you will encounter examples of virtually every important business technique — goal setting, coping with cultural change, managing resources, trimming overhead, aligning priorities, performing quality assurance, improving quality, benchmarking, undertaking competitive analysis, managing by fact — you name it, and it's here.

You'll also encounter models of superb corporate skill. Although the leadership and management styles of these ten successful current and former head coaches may vary, the results don't. These people understand the art of winning. The men we meet in these pages are not just successful leaders, they are interesting people.

The raw energy of Mike Ditka radiates off the page, for example, as do the wit, compassion, and common sense of Bud Grant and the no-nonsense practicality of Chuck Noll. Though Ditka, Grant, and Noll have radically different approaches to the game and their roles, all are enshrined in the Pro Football Hall of Fame. The fundamental values that anchor them, as well as the seven other successful coaches here, encompass traits to which every business leader today should aspire:

· Professional competence — they know what they're doing
· A love of their work — they enjoy what they're doing
· A sense of stewardship — they act to perpetuate the organization and the sport

coaches, general managers, and owners come and go, but the game and the teams remain relevant. In fact, this constant reordering of talent and resources may be the key to the NFL's staying power both as a sport and as a business. At the team level, when one combination of players, coaches, and strategies stops working, another is employed — then another, and another, until a winning combination is found.

Contrast this with the inertia and timidity of many Fortune 500 companies that have fallen on hard times in recent years. When things stopped working, they suppressed the data; denied the problem; and blamed their advertising agencies, their competitors, the government, even their customers, rather than own up to their responsibility as leaders and stewards of the corporation.

Another of the great strengths of the NFL, and the source of much of its appeal, is that it is a pure meritocracy. Every season each team must renew itself and perform against the top talent in the sport. No amount of favoritism, politics, residual influence, or political action money can alter the need for measurable performance. Failure to win, or at least be competitive, can result in changes in players, coaches, management, or whatever else is required to get the team back on track. This may be the ultimate form of zero-based budgeting.

Indeed, one of the most challenging aspects of football, or, for that matter, any professional team sport, is the reality that change and renewal are the only constants. A team may achieve extraordinary success, make the playoffs, even win the Super Bowl. Yet, with the beginning of each new season, that same team must return to the first step in an annual process of analysis, redefinition, and strategic examination founded upon the value system and basic principles that have made it successful before. It must return to the root of its potential.

"I was; therefore, I am" is not an adage you will find within the language of the successful team. "I was, but that doesn't mean a thing this season" is a more likely turn of phrase.

Understanding and mastering such an accelerated renewal

- A capacity to lead — they make tough decisions in the common interest
- An ability to motivate and inspire loyalty — they know how to get the best from their personnel

The themes and lessons contained in this book are timeless. Strong leadership always has been about making the whole greater than the sum of its parts. Self-sacrifice, competence, hard work, loyalty, and acceptance of nothing less than the best from each member of a group are not new ideas. Neither are setting targets and inspiring people to achieve them. Successful leaders throughout history all have employed such tools to one degree or another. Knowing when to switch strategies, when to take risks, and how to build and rebuild are universal requirements of leadership in sports, business, politics, or life.

What makes this book so pertinent is that the coaches featured here have done these things so consistently well. Just as importantly, they have done them in an organizational environment that is virtual, fast-moving, and unbelievably demanding — in short, a twenty-first-century context.

In a world thirsting for new leadership models, *Game Plans for Success* contains invaluable examples of successful, postmodern management in action. Consider it as a universally applicable series of philosophies on the powerful potential of pure teamwork, both on the field of sport and in the fields of commerce and industry. Teamwork creates knowledge and performance that are both profound and compelling; it remains the central element of all human achievement.

Creating a Winning Environment

Marty Schottenheimer

HEAD COACH

KANSAS CITY CHIEFS, 1989—PRESENT

The Kansas City Chiefs were a struggling football team before Marty Schottenheimer arrived in 1989. The club had sunk to the bottom of the AFC and showed no signs of rising.

Schottenheimer changed all that. In his first season as head coach, he led the Chiefs to a winning record, 8–7–1. In his second season he guided the team to eleven victories, its best showing in twenty-one years.

"I didn't know what the NFL was all about until Marty came to Kansas City," says Chiefs defensive tackle Bill Maas. "I never knew how unorganized we were until I saw how Marty did things. He put the whole thing together for us."

"I've only worked with one head coach who had as great a total understanding of football as Marty, and that was Tom Landry," says quarterback Steve DeBerg. "Marty could teach any phase of the game and coach it successfully."

Schottenheimer, fifty-one, has been a head coach for ten full seasons, five in Cleveland (including one partial season) and six in Kansas City. He has not had a losing record. His overall career record is 108–72–1, and his nine playoff appearances since 1985 are a record unmatched by any other NFL coach. Under

Schottenheimer, the Chiefs reached double figures in victories four consecutive seasons (1990–93), a franchise first.

Schottenheimer did not merely revitalize the Chiefs. He helped revitalize the community. An NFL game in Kansas City now is a major event for fans, most of whom are clad in team colors at packed Arrowhead Stadium. The Chiefs' home attendance hit an all-time high in 1994. Kansas City averaged just 50,000 fans per game in 1988; it led the league in 1994 with an average home attendance of 76,734.

"Marty came here with a winning attitude, and that was something new," cornerback Albert Lewis says. "It's like being a golfer and seeing nothing but sand traps. That's what it was like before Marty came here. Now all we see are greens."

Born in Canonsburg, Pennsylvania, Schottenheimer was an All-America linebacker at the University of Pittsburgh. He played six years in the American Football League with the Buffalo Bills (1965–68) and the Boston Patriots (1969–70). He retired in 1971 but then came back to play with Portland in the World Football League in 1974.

When an injury sidelined him in Portland, Schottenheimer volunteered to coach the linebackers. The following year he landed a job as an assistant coach with the NFL's New York Giants. Schottenheimer has been coaching in the NFL ever since.

Schottenheimer led Cleveland to two AFC Championship Games, but lost to Denver each time. He left the Browns following the 1988 season and signed with the Chiefs.

"Marty has all the traits of a great coach," says Carl Peterson, the Chiefs' president and general manager. "He is tremendously well-organized, he has the respect of his players, and he is an outstanding motivator."

"Marty keeps everything constant," adds Maas, who played with the Chiefs from 1984 through 1992. "He works so damn hard during the week that you would go out and do anything for him on Sunday. He is a man's man and a player's coach."

S ometimes I'm amazed when I consider the course my life has taken.

I'm a career football coach, having spent the last twenty years in the business. Yet there was a time when coaching was the last thing I wanted to do.

My NFL playing career ended on a sour note. I was traded twice and cut once in a period of three months in 1971. I had no illusions about my playing ability. I was a journeyman linebacker at the pro level. But two trades and a release in three months was more rejection than I was prepared to accept.

I was almost twenty-eight years old when head coach Don McCafferty cut me in Baltimore before the 1971 season. I did not have any job prospects. At the time, some people asked whether I would consider coaching, but I rejected the idea. I said there was absolutely no way I would get into coaching. There was no security. Coaches bounced around even more than players, and I had done enough bouncing around already. I did not want to subject my family to that kind of life. I was getting out.

I settled in Denver with my wife, Pat, and our newborn daughter, Kristen. I got into the real-estate business. But, as time passed, I found I missed football.

There is competition in real estate, but it isn't like football. There is nothing like the emotional rush of game day or the satisfaction that follows a big win.

I began visiting the Denver Broncos' office and hanging out with Joe Collier, who was the defensive coordinator. I had the itch to get back in the game, but I didn't know how.

One day the head coach, John Ralston, asked about my career aspirations. I still remember my answer. I said, "I'm going to become a head coach in the National Football League." Just like that, my career path changed.

That statement must have seemed arrogant coming from a real-estate salesman who had not coached a day in his life, but that was how I felt. Ralston, a career football man himself, understood.

The World Football League was born just about that time. Collier put me in touch with Dick Coury, head coach of the Portland team. I asked Coury if he needed a linebackers coach. Like most WFL teams, Portland was operating on a shoestring budget and could not afford to have a separate coach dedicated specifically to linebackers.

"But we'll sign you as a player," Coury said.

It was a crazy thing to even consider. I was thirty-one. I had been out of the game for three years. And I had no idea whether this new league would last a month. But it was a chance to get back into football.

I discussed it with Pat. I said, "If I want to get into coaching, I think I have to do this."

She supported me, although I'm sure she had serious doubts about my sanity.

I played a few games in Portland and then was sidelined with a shoulder injury. Rather than stand around and do nothing at practice, I offered to coach the linebackers. And that was how I broke into coaching. Although the WFL did not last, my career as a coach has.

I've been a head coach in the NFL for eleven years, five in Cleveland and the last six in Kansas City. My teams have won four division titles and qualified for the playoffs nine times.

I still have not coached in a Super Bowl, and that goal is what drives me — the desire to take a team to the top, to be the very best.

I've been close. In Cleveland we went to the AFC Championship Game twice — and each time we lost close games to Denver. In 1993 our Kansas City team went to the championship game but then lost to Buffalo. We've been one step away from the Super Bowl three times.

It is disappointing; but if it had come easily, I'm not sure I would have known how to handle it.

Persistence Pays

If my life in football, especially coaching, represents anything, it is the value of persistence. It took me a while to figure out that a career in coaching was what I wanted; but once I came to that realization, I didn't let go.

I hear businesspeople talk about the risk involved in new ventures, the fear that overtakes a corporation when the profit margin drops and there is talk of a cutback. I spent enough time in business to know the pressure concerning the bottom line is every bit as real as the pressure felt by a coach or player in the NFL.

But I reached a point after the WFL folded when I was flat broke. I had to decide whether to stay in football and continue to pursue this coaching dream or to do what most people would consider the sensible thing, go back into the real-estate business. I had fifty-five dollars in the bank. My mother-in-law had to send money so we could buy Christmas presents for the kids.

That was one of those moments when you have to face yourself, to look in the mirror and say, "Okay, what's it gonna be?" I made the decision to stay in football. Pat stood by me and, in fact, helped get me back into the game. Pat wants to write a book about our marriage. She already has the title: "Football, for Better or Worse."

Here's a story that should give you some idea of the lengths I went to in order to stay in pro football.

In January 1975 I went to the Senior Bowl in Mobile, Alabama, where the pro coaches and scouts gather to see the top college prospects. I went hoping to land a coaching job. Because I didn't have any money, I shared a room with an old friend, Richie McCabe, then a coach with Buffalo.

I met Bill Arnsparger, who was then head coach of the New York Giants. He didn't have any openings on his staff, but he asked me whether I would write a report on talent in the World Football League. The WFL was going broke, and the NFL teams wanted to get a line on the best players in order to sign them.

The offer, I thought, was for fifteen hundred dollars, which seemed like all the money in the world at the time. More important, it was my chance to impress Arnsparger with my football expertise and possibly pave the way for a coaching job.

I went over every WFL game film I could get my hands on. I wrote my report, ranking the top 100 players by position. Pat sat next to me and typed each page. If she made the slightest mistake, even one letter, I made her type the whole page over again.

I sent the finished report to Arnsparger, and he sent back a letter of thanks with a check for $125. I later found out we had a misunderstanding about my fee.

According to Bill, he said he would pay "fifty or a hundred dollars" for the report.

I thought he had said "fifteen hundred dollars."

By paying $125, Arnsparger was giving me what he considered the maximum, plus a little extra for content and neatness.

I was disappointed but never mentioned it to Bill until years later. Although Pat and I could have used the money, the important thing was that Arnsparger knew who I was. A month later he called and said he was looking for a linebackers coach.

That was my big break.

I was an assistant coach with the Giants for three years and then spent two seasons in Detroit before joining the Cleveland Browns as defensive coordinator in 1980. I was named head coach of the Browns in October 1984 and have been a head coach ever since.

I left Cleveland following the 1988 season because of a disagreement with owner Art Modell (which I'll discuss in more detail later). Then I was hired by the Chiefs. I've never been happier, working for the man I consider the best owner in all of sports, Lamar Hunt, and with an outstanding general manager, Carl Peterson.

In Kansas City I've had the opportunity to coach two of

the greatest players of all time: quarterback Joe Montana and running back Marcus Allen. Our team went to the playoffs every season from 1990 to 1994. No other club in the NFL can make that claim.

Raise the Expectation Level

In business they call it a lateral move when you go from one company to another and stay in the same position. It generally is not viewed as a positive thing. Why move to a new corporation when it means having the same job? Most executives make a move only when it involves a promotion and a fat raise.

My situation was different, because I left Cleveland and was looking for another job when I joined the Chiefs. But it was, in effect, a lateral move because I went to Kansas City as head coach — not head coach and general manager, not head coach and team president, not head coach and part-owner.

The sign on my door was exactly the same and so were my duties. Only the team I worked for had changed.

For me, the lateral move could not have worked out better, although many people felt I was stepping into a hopeless situation in Kansas City. I believed otherwise and took the job determined to prove that the Chiefs could make a comeback.

True, the Chiefs had been down for a long time. After the team won Super Bowl IV in January 1970, it didn't win another postseason game for two decades. From 1974 through 1988 the Chiefs had only two winning seasons — not to mention six head coaches.

Attendance at Arrowhead Stadium declined along with the record. The average home attendance had slipped almost 40 percent; season-ticket sales were among the lowest in the league.

Contrast that with the situation I left in Cleveland, where the team was a championship contender and the stadium was packed for every home game. The difference was like night and day.

I shocked a great many people when I came to Kansas City and said, "I believe we can win very, very quickly."

I did not say it to sell tickets or make the evening news. I said it because I believed it. My belief later was borne out on the field. In our first year the Chiefs won eight games, doubling the total of the previous season.

My prediction did not require any great leap of faith on my part, although it probably seemed so. I simply referred to the situation in Cleveland. The Browns were a last-place team when I took over as head coach. The next year we made the playoffs.

I turned that team around; I saw no reason why I couldn't turn around the Chiefs. You have to raise the level of expectation — not your own level, but that of the people around you. Always aim high.

It was a different city, a different team, a different ownership. But, for me, it was the same job. I noted the differences between the two situations but didn't view them as negatives in relation to my new position.

More than anything, I was excited by the challenge.

One thing I've found is that moving from one organization to another brings a tremendous surge in energy. You're filled with anticipation. The challenges are new, possibly greater, but at the same time there is this energy you can draw upon.

So a lateral move can be a positive thing if you approach it that way. Keep an open mind. Accept the fact that things are bound to be different in any job switch. Perhaps they will not be as good at the outset, which certainly was the case going from the Browns to the Chiefs. But take the excitement you feel and pump it back into the organization. Make it work for you.

Keep in mind, however, that just because you are changing addresses doesn't mean you have to change your approach. When another organization takes the bold step of hiring you, as the Chiefs did with me, they have said, in effect, "We believe in you."

What the new group is looking for is essentially what you

delivered before. It would be a mistake for an executive to make a lateral move, one company to another, and suddenly decide that because he is in a new situation, he should blaze a new trail.

With few exceptions, I go about my job now the same way I always have. I believe in doing things the same way. I still think the most important aspects of coaching are credibility, trust, and communication. If you have those things going for you in football, you'll win. And if you have them going for you as a business executive, you will win, too. They are the fundamental building blocks to success in any field.

I believe that when you come in as a new head coach or manager, especially from another team or firm, the high point of your credibility is right at the outset.

Some people may disagree and say there is a trial stage where the new guy has to prove himself, but I don't believe that. Assuming the new head coach or manager has a winning background, as I did in Cleveland, he will find the new group receptive and eager to hear what he has to say.

As the new guy, you represent change, a new voice, a fresh outlook. NFL players always are looking for ways to improve. They will listen closely to what you have to say, especially at the first meeting.

If you make a strong impression, if you spell out your program with clarity and confidence, you will have the team solidly behind you. If you come across as vague and un-focused, you create doubt in the minds of the players. Remember, they are looking for something substantial. Give it to them.

I told the Chiefs' players the same thing I told the press: we could be a winning team. I said I thought we could compete for a playoff spot. Those not only were positive but, I believed, realistic goals.

I went through it point by point with the players: how the Chiefs stacked up against the competition, where they were lacking the previous season and by how much.

My point was that we weren't that far away from being a

playoff contender. We had some good young players but had a lot of work to do. I compared it to climbing a ladder: the idea is to reach the top, but we had to take it one step at a time.

For a new head coach or corporate executive to make a lot of grandiose promises is dangerous, because at some point he will be held accountable. If you don't deliver, you lose credibility.

I identify concrete objectives that I feel our team has at least a 70 to 75 percent chance of achieving. I don't make them too low, because why aim low? I don't want to put them out of sight, either. Players know the difference. If the goals aren't properly set, they lose meaning.

But if the goals are achievable — X number of take-aways on defense, X number of rushing yards on offense — and you, as head coach, say, "Reach these objectives and we'll win," and it all comes together, then you've really got something. It is called affirmation.

At that point, the team really believes in your program. People will leap to whatever you put on the board next because they trust that you know their capabilities and that you know how to turn those capabilities into victories.

You are not going to bat 1.000; no one does. But if you come out ahead most of the time, that's all anyone can expect.

One thing that was helpful in making the move from Cleveland to Kansas City was that I brought most of my staff with me. I brought nine people — eight assistant coaches and an equipment manager. That was a tremendous help because we already understood each other and spoke the same language.

I would not have been so bold in talking about winning the first year if I hadn't had that staff in place. Continuity is important in football, just as it is in business.

If I had hired eight new coaches, I would have spent months getting them up to speed with my system — and that period would have meant time lost working with the players. With our staff intact, we were able to hit the ground running.

Another thing we had going for us was the tradition of the

Chiefs. In the 1960s Kansas City was one of the dominant franchises in the American Football League. It was a team with great pride, a team that had won three AFL titles and sent six men to the Pro Football Hall of Fame.

A number of former players still lived in the Kansas City area, but many had become disenchanted with the team and its losing ways. One of the first things Peterson and I did was reach out to those players. We had them attend games. We had them visit our locker room. We had them travel with the team.

It was the best way we could think of to combat the losing image the Chiefs had built up over twenty years. We could point to the former players and their history of success in Kansas City and use it as a reference point for our young players.

People did backflips when we won eight games in 1989, but I wasn't that surprised.

If you look at the NFL standings each season, many teams are able to win eight or nine games. And every year, there are two or three teams that are clearly better than everyone else. At the other end of the scale, there are three or four teams that are really down and out. That leaves a large group of twenty to twenty-three teams that are pretty much the same. So the question is, What separates the teams that win nine or ten games and make the playoffs from the teams that win six games and fall short?

I contend that if you have a good organization and take care of the basics, a team can be in that playoff group almost every year.

Too often head coaches lose sight of what's important. They think the answer lies in a radical new offense or a million-dollar free agent, when success really comes with doing the little things right day after day.

A front office that is efficient and a coaching staff that knows how to communicate create an atmosphere that allows the athletes to perform at their best. With that atmosphere in place, you win.

If you want to step up to the elite class, among the top two or three teams, you have to make bolder moves, such as the ones we made signing Allen and trading for Montana in 1993. We had a solid team and organization, but we believed those guys could take us to the next level.

Take a winning system and add a dynamic player with championship experience, and you are armed to make a run at the Super Bowl. We came up just short in 1993, winning two playoff rounds before losing the AFC Championship Game in Buffalo.

Winning is not an accident. You can win an occasional game on a lucky bounce or a fluke play. But winning on a consistent basis, whether in football or in business, requires planning and organization.

I call it a "winning environment," and as head coach, it is something I must create before I hope to achieve anything else. A winning environment is generated by three basic principles: first, you must be able to identify what you want to achieve. It is virtually impossible for anyone to achieve an objective unless you are 100 percent sure of what it is. Second, you must be able to communicate your ideas to the group. Third, you must be able, as a practical matter, to turn those ideas into reality.

As the head coach or corporate head, you must present these objectives to the group in such a way that each individual sees them as important. There was a time when a leader could get results by saying, "Do this because I say so." That approach falls flat today.

The effective manager now presents his objectives so that the individual — in my case, the player — adopts the objectives as his own. If he sees the value, he will put forth a better effort.

It is impossible for you to achieve my goal for me. The only way you and I can get where we want to go is if we have the same goal and work toward it together. We may disagree about how to get there. But as long as we have the same goal, we have a good chance of reaching it.

It is a different world out there today. People aren't as inclined to follow, and they certainly won't follow blindly. A typical worker is quick to ask, "What's in it for me?" He might not say it aloud, but that's the thought process. Self-interest is a basic principle on which we all operate. As a head coach, I have to accept that and find a way to use it within a team concept to get where I want to go.

The key is to make the answer to "What's in it for me?" common to everyone.

With our team, as simplistic as it may sound, I talk about winning a championship. I ask the players, "What is it that you want out of this game?"

Even in this era of million-dollar free agents, most of the players still want the same thing: to win the NFL championship. You saw that principle in action the past few seasons when some players, such as Deion Sanders, went to a certain team when they could have signed for more money elsewhere. Why? Because they wanted a Super Bowl ring.

I lay that out for our guys. I say, "I know what you're thinking. An NFL championship is what it's all about. But none of you can get there alone. Together, we can do it."

It is when you lose that focus, when forty guys start playing for their individual bonuses and next year's free-agent contracts, that you wind up with everyone going in different directions. They are putting out an effort, but it isn't accomplishing a thing for the team because it isn't focused.

Football is a people business, which is one of the reasons I love it so much. But any business can work better if the people at the top create an atmosphere that acknowledges the workers as people, not inventory.

It doesn't matter whether you are in football, real estate, or electronics, the people who work for you will be happier and more productive if they feel they have value to you beyond what they can do for you on the job. They want to feel that they are important on a personal level.

It all comes back to the value of communication. When there is no communication between the head of a business and his workforce, there is no understanding. The boss winds up with some kind of crisis and asks, "How did this happen?"

The answer is easy: he lost touch.

I make a point of telling my people that my office door always is open. If they have a problem, they can discuss it with me. If something is bothering a player, whether it is a football matter or trouble at home, I want to help if I can. My basic message is, "You're important to me and not just for what you do on the field."

But saying your door is open is just a start. That puts the worker in the position of having to come to you. And some players are not comfortable doing that.

With the Chiefs, we take it a step further. We go into the locker room and the administrative office to gather insight and gain perspective. I'm not afraid to ask a player, "Are you okay with this short-yardage play? What would you like to do?"

Carl Peterson does the same thing with the people in our executive office, whether they work in marketing, public relations, data processing, or ticket sales. We're always asking our people, "What do you think? How do you feel about this?"

It accomplishes two things: you acquire the opinions of your people, which are valuable, and you give your employees a chance to feel that they really are a part of the big picture. If a worker feels he has a hand in shaping how things are done, he will be more excited about being involved.

The more people who have a sense of ownership and leadership in a project, the higher the level of motivation. It is when people feel disconnected from the whole that they question whether their efforts matter. That's when they start going through the motions.

The Bond of Trust

The foundation of getting people to do what you want them to do is built on a relationship based on trust. That is the critical element, the glue that holds everything together.

It is like marriage. You and your wife might disagree on

any number of issues, but if you each trust that the other party is after a good marriage, you probably will have a good marriage. Trust holds things together.

It also is true in an organization.

As an individual, you don't have to agree with the means by which an end is achieved. As long as all parties trust that everyone is after the same thing, success can follow.

We see it in football all the time. Certain players wish they had bigger roles. But as long as they believe in the overall program, the job gets done.

In pro football trust is tied directly to team ownership and management. Players want to believe — *need* to believe — that winning is as important to the front office as it is to the guys on the field.

If they don't believe that, they will find it hard to give their best effort.

Players make great sacrifices to play this game. They spend long hours training and studying. They take a tremendous beating and live with pain on a daily basis. It is hard for them to pay that price if they don't believe team management has the same commitment to winning.

Ownership can demonstrate its commitment in several ways. It can spend big money to sign the top free agents. It can ensure that the team has a modern training facility with a good practice field and weight room. Those things help to create the winning environment I mentioned earlier.

But if you're a player and you see your all-pro teammates leaving to sign for more money elsewhere, and you are practicing on a dumpy field, then you read that the owner is cutting the scouting staff to save money, how are you likely to feel?

Most players would say, "Why should I break my butt to win this game? The front office doesn't care. Why should *I* care?"

Sometimes this situation gets twisted. Players may try to deflect the blame for their own failures by putting the blame on the owner, the head coach, or other players.

When I came to Kansas City, I found that kind of finger-pointing. I wasn't surprised. When a team has had two winning seasons in fifteen years, there is a lot of blame to be shared.

One of the first things I did with the Chiefs was to sit down with each player, one-on-one, to get a sense of what he was thinking. Bill Maas, an outstanding defensive tackle, was among the first.

Bill went on and on about how the Chiefs' organization wasn't willing to do this and that. He talked about how his teammates weren't as committed to winning as he was.

Finally I said, "Bill, let me tell you something. I respect how you feel, but you have to understand something. You are not charged with the responsibility of deciding whether player A, B, C, or D is as committed to winning as you are. That's my call as head coach."

I told Maas his responsibility was to continue his commitment to being the best player he could be and to trust — there's that word again — that the other members of the organization, including me, would create an environment in which we could be successful.

I said I wasn't familiar with what happened on the Chiefs before my arrival, but I assured him that Mr. Hunt was committed to doing everything in his power to put the team back on track.

I asked Bill to give me some time to put the pieces together. I said, "If you can't do that, you become part of the problem, not part of the solution." To his credit, Bill responded and played very well for us.

I approached a number of other players in the same fashion. I listened to their concerns. I asked for their trust in the new management team. And, once they gave it, their level of play improved dramatically.

We did a few other things that first year, such as bringing in some veterans with winning backgrounds. We acquired Ron Jaworski, who quarterbacked the Eagles to Super Bowl XV, and Mike Webster, the center who played on all four Pittsburgh Steelers championship teams. Their leadership was a real plus.

But the bottom line is winning games, of course.

I could have talked about change until I was blue in the face, and it wouldn't have meant a thing if we hadn't shown improvement on the field. Once we started to win a few games — and we won a big one early against the Raiders, 24–19 — the whole organization, top to bottom, pulled closer together.

We've built on that foundation ever since. Between 1990 and 1994 our regular-season record was 51–29, second only to Buffalo in the AFC. We developed a solid core of veterans, players we acquired and developed in our system. Unlike the group we inherited, these guys know how to win.

Seek Leadership from Within

What I see on this team now is great leadership. As a head coach or a department head, you want that to develop. The most successful teams that I've been around were those where the players drove the machine.

I'm not talking about during the game. I'm talking about in the locker room, in the meeting room, and on the practice field. Certain standards were set. And they weren't set by the coaches as much as they were by the players themselves. There was a level of expectation in terms of preparation, effort, and so forth. If certain players fell short, the other guys were quick to say, "Get with it."

That direction is much more effective coming from another player than coming from a coach. Players get tired of listening to coaches. When the guy at the next locker verbally kicks a player in the butt, it makes an impression.

Once a team develops that kind of mind-set and each player knows that every other player has worked as hard, studied as hard, and trained as hard as he himself has leading up to a game, it is much easier to execute well on the field. The trust factor is clearly defined.

That trust means the defensive end never has to look over his shoulder to see whether the linebacker is covering his back. It means the cornerback doesn't have to worry about whether the safety will be there to help him in pass coverage. He knows the safety will be there, just as the safety knows the cornerback will be where he is supposed to be.

A coach can scream and holler about teamwork, but the teams that really have it are the ones on which the players live it and demand it every day. It comes with mutual respect and internal leadership.

You have this type of leadership in business, too. Often it is the people in middle management who make sure that things get done, that everyone carries his share of the load. When you have that leadership at the middle level, chances are you will operate efficiently — because those people are closer to the situation than the guys upstairs.

To give a perfect example, Joe Montana served a middle-management role with our team in 1994. He set the tempo in practice. He worked with our offensive coordinator in putting together the game plan. Joe didn't make us a better team just on Sunday, he made us a better team *every* day of the week. We miss him.

That type of leadership in the locker room makes my job easier. The players already are well-motivated, so I just have to point them in the right direction. I do that by setting goals.

I set both long- and short-term goals for the team. The long-term goal, obviously, is to win a Super Bowl. We begin each season with that as our objective.

But in football you play a game every week, so you have to set short-term goals to keep the players focused. Each week we have goals based on what we need to do to win that particular game. Then each Monday, we go over the results: "We met this goal — good job. We didn't meet this one. All right, we know what we have to work on." It couldn't be more clear-cut.

But good week or bad, we reinforce the overall idea. We are here to do one thing, and that's win a Super Bowl. We don't lose sight of that goal. Ever.

The worst thing that can be done by a head coach or team management is to arbitrarily establish a goal that is well beneath the team's capability.

Let's say you set your team goal as making the playoffs. If you do make it, half the players will be drinking champagne in the locker room because they reached the goal. Now how do you get them ready to play another game? It is very difficult.

So while it is a healthy thing to establish goals for your team or employees, you must establish those goals with care and a lot of thought.

Earlier I mentioned leaving Cleveland following the 1988 season in a disagreement with the owner, Art Modell. Art and I were good friends and remain good friends. At that point we just didn't see things the same way on a particular issue.

Modell was not satisfied with some of the people on my coaching staff, and he wanted to make changes. While I recognized his right to feel that way, I pointed out that we had achieved quite a bit in four seasons as a staff, going to the playoffs each year.

Art and I discussed the matter, and he was quite adamant in his views. I happen to feel very strongly that the sole responsibility for the selection and administration of the coaching staff should belong to the head coach.

It was a difficult situation, because I have great regard for Modell. He gave me the opportunity to be a head coach, and I'll always be grateful for that. But this was a case where we were not going to agree.

After much discussion, Art and I decided it would be in everyone's best interest if we parted company. It was a hard thing to do, because I spent nine years in Cleveland as a coach and my two children grew up there. But I knew it was for the best.

So the question arose, What's my next move? I almost took a coordinator's job with another team, but the head-coach position opened in Kansas City. One visit with Hunt and Peterson was enough to convince me that this was a great opportunity.

It was a lateral move, but a lateral move that made all the sense in the world. I felt comfortable working with Peterson. He is a former coach, having served on Dick Vermeil's staff in Philadelphia. He understands the game and knows how to evaluate players. We work well together.

When I moved from Cleveland to Kansas City and brought along almost my entire staff, people asked if that meant I would do everything exactly the same — keep the same schedule, follow the same practice routine, work from the same playbook.

The answers were yes and no.

I don't believe in changing for the sake of change. We had good success with a formula in Cleveland, and I didn't see the need to make a whole lot of changes just because we were in a new organization.

Our overall approach and our basic offensive and defensive philosophy remained the same. Within that framework we made adjustments, as we would in any season. However, we didn't set out to reinvent our program. The people who do that, both in football and in business, often wind up going backward.

Of course, there is no such thing as a static environment. Things around us change all the time. In the NFL rules are rewritten, new teams are formed, and players move from team to team as free agents. In business, interest rates fluctuate, corporations merge, and technology continues to explode.

For management, the question becomes, "What do we need to do differently to keep pace?" Change too little, and you get left behind. Change too much, and you can veer off-course. It is a balancing act that, as a head coach, I find becomes trickier every year.

We made changes in our first six seasons in Kansas City. For example, we went to the playoffs with three different quarterbacks: Steve DeBerg, David Krieg, and Montana. Each quarterback had his own strengths and weaknesses, which forced us to modify the offense in some areas and allowed us to open it up in others.

The pro game has become more of a passing game, especially with recent rules changes. In 1994 our team attempted 615 passes, which was almost a club record, but that did not mean we stopped running the ball. Acquiring Allen and using our top draft pick in 1994 on Greg Hill, a running back from Texas A & M, prove that we still are committed to a strong running game.

Too much tinkering is a dangerous thing. I say that, yet I'm guilty of it myself.

In 1994 I changed the way our team worked at training camp. I backed off on the physical aspect. We did less scrimmaging and less contact work.

It went against my nature as a coach who believes in the physical approach, but I did it in response to the new rules regarding a salary cap. Each NFL team now has only so much money to spend on players, so you literally cannot afford to have players injured. If you use all the money under your salary cap and have players who are hurt and cannot play, you cannot sign other players to replace them.

With that in mind, I cut back on the hitting in our training camp. I thought it would reduce the chance of injury in the preseason, and I hoped it would keep our players fresher for the long haul of the regular season.

As it turned out, I was wrong on both counts.

Our injuries more than doubled in 1994. Our starters missed a combined total of thirty-six games, twenty-three on offense and thirteen on defense. We also lost several close games, including two by a single point and another in overtime. I believe those are games that we would have won in previous seasons.

We lost some of the physical and mental toughness that you must have to be successful in this league. I trace some of that to the changes I made in our training camp. We did not build the intensity we had in previous years. So in future training camps, we are back to regular hitting.

As a coach or business executive, you must be willing to try new ideas. The changes in the game and business demand flexibility. But I believe there are certain absolutes that you should not stray too far from — because if you do, you lose the foundation for what you are trying to achieve.

A danger I see in business — and football definitely is a business — is that the demands on the head coach or head of the company are multiplying daily. In many cases the demands take you, as the boss, away from your area of expertise and into areas in which you may not be that well-versed.

This is a major problem. I never wanted the administrative aspect of my job to take away from what I'm paid to do — which is to coach. That is why I was happy to be a head coach, and a head coach only, in Cleveland and Kansas City. I was more than willing to let someone like Peterson sit in the general manager's chair and handle administrative matters.

But it has become almost impossible to stay away from them. The nature of the game today demands that head coaches take on added responsibilities in the areas of free agency, talent evaluation, and administration. I did it grudgingly at first but now have accepted it.

I can sympathize with an advertising executive or architect who loves his craft, but then finds himself promoted to head of a department. Suddenly he is spending his whole day in conferences. He is not doing what he feels he does best, whether it is coming up with an ad campaign or designing an office building.

It can be frustrating, but I also know I have no choice but to do administrative things — so I try to organize my time and not let the football part of my job get away from me. I allot time to those other matters but make sure the bulk of my time still is devoted to coaching.

It is hard to believe I've been doing this for more than twenty years. I was a guy who wanted no part of coaching, yet I'm now so deeply immersed in it I cannot imagine doing anything else.

We had great times in Cleveland in the 1980s. The town had taken so much abuse over the years, with comedians calling it the "mistake on the lake" and such. The people there were looking for something they could feel good about, and in the Browns we gave them a team they could rally around.

I'll never forget the feeling of walking off that field on a Sunday after a big win, seeing the pride in people's faces. It was gratifying beyond words. We saw the same thing when we turned this franchise around in Kansas City.

I've been asked many times about the two heartbreaking losses to the Broncos in the AFC playoffs. In the first game Denver quarterback John Elway led his team ninety-eight yards to the tying touchdown in the final minute. The Broncos then kicked a field goal in overtime to beat us. In the second game we appeared on the verge of winning when our best running back, Earnest Byner, fumbled near the Denver goal line.

People ask how I came back from those two losses.

The way I see it, if you are willing to open your arms and accept the euphoria of victory, you have to be willing to accept the other side. We beat the New York Jets in a double-overtime game to advance to our first conference championship against Denver, so that was my time to celebrate. The next week brought the fall.

My mother always told me there are two ways of dealing with hardship. You can close your eyes and hope it goes away, which does not accomplish anything. Or you can roll up your sleeves and attack the problem.

I've often compared it to learning how to ride a bicycle. As long as you are willing to get back on when you fall off and start pedaling again, you can get where you want to go. If you leave the bicycle on the ground, you won't go anywhere.

The Importance of Preparation

Joe Gibbs

HEAD COACH

WASHINGTON REDSKINS, 1981–92

Joe Gibbs did more than just take his team to four Super Bowls in twelve seasons as head coach of the Washington Redskins. He earned the respect of his players and his peers in the coaching profession as an honest, straightforward person.

"Here's a man with all this power and yet he never throws it in your face," says Charles Mann, a former all-pro defensive end with the Redskins. "A coach is supposed to be above his players, but Coach Gibbs talked with you on your level."

"Coach Gibbs is not a good man, he's a great man," says tight end Don Warren. "He's a player's coach. He's not a dictator who believes there is only one way to do things."

Gibbs retired from coaching after the 1992 NFL season, citing the stress brought on by years of 100-hour work weeks. During the season, Gibbs often slept in his office three nights a week. He prepared for a game the way Allied generals prepared for D-Day, covering every last detail.

Gibbs compiled a 124–60 regular-season record in Washington, and his playoff record of 16–5 is the third best in NFL history. He won three Super Bowls with three different quarterbacks: Joe Theismann (XVII), Doug Williams (XXII), and Mark Rypien (XXVI).

Gibbs was born in Mocksville, North Carolina, the son of a policeman. The family moved to California, where as a teenager Gibbs developed a love of auto racing. Today, he owns a NASCAR racing team based in Charlotte, North Carolina. He also appears as an analyst on NBC's telecasts of NFL games.

Gibbs played college football at San Diego State under head coach Don Coryell, who later hired Gibbs as an assistant coach at San Diego State and then brought him along to the St. Louis Cardinals and the San Diego Chargers. Gibbs spent seventeen years as an assistant at four colleges and with three NFL teams before he was given a chance to be a head coach in Washington.

A modest man, Gibbs often jokes about his low-key personality. His typical postgame celebration consisted of a hamburger and an evening in front of the television with his wife, Pat, and sons, J. D. and Coy. After Super Bowls, he would treat himself to chocolate sundaes.

Gibbs also pokes fun at his athletic skills. He says that when he went to San Diego State as a coach, the first thing he did was burn the film from his own playing career there. In truth, Gibbs is a fine athlete, good enough to win the national over–thirty-five racquetball title in 1976.

Beneath his quiet exterior, Gibbs was one of the NFL's fiercest competitors. The bigger the game, the better he coached — and the better his team usually played, as reflected in his postseason record.

"He doesn't give you any bull," wide receiver Gary Clark says of Gibbs. "He lays it out for you. When he tells you something, you know you've heard the straight story. He doesn't try to trick you the way some coaches do."

Gibbs also has made his mark on the NASCAR circuit. In 1993 his team finished fourth in the Winston Cup standings and won the series' most prestigious race, the Daytona 500. His racing team is sponsored by Interstate Batteries, with NFL Properties as an associate sponsor.

A deeply religious man, Gibbs is actively involved in community service with Christian outreach programs.

There is an old football saying: The will to win is meaningless without the will to prepare.

That is so true.

Everyone wants to win on game day. Every coach and player walks on the field fired up and raring to go. But if they have not put in the time to prepare during the week, they will fall flat on their faces.

A winning effort begins with preparation. The game may be played on Sunday, but it is won on the practice field during the week; in the meeting rooms, where coaches and players prepare the game plan; and in the weight room, where the best players do a few extra repetitions.

That's where the will comes in.

It's easy to be motivated on game day with sixty thousand people in the stands and millions watching on TV. But it's harder to push yourself through the third hour of practice on a Wednesday, or to take film home at night. That takes a little extra. Yet that extra effort may decide who wins on Sunday.

Trying to win in the NFL without preparation is like trying to pass the bar exam without going to class. Talent is meaningless unless you invest the time and effort to prepare.

I'm a stickler for preparation. I was that way as a football coach, and I'm that way now as owner of a NASCAR racing team. In football and racing, there's always an element of chance. But with good preparation, you greatly reduce the margin for error.

When I coached the Washington Redskins, my shortest workday was game day. Sunday was a breeze compared with the rest of the week. I worked sixteen hours a day, sometimes more. I slept in my office three nights a week. During the season, I left home on Monday morning and did not return until Thursday night.

I'm not saying everyone should work the way I did. The strain all those hours put on me and my family led to my decision to retire from the NFL after the 1992 season. But that approach was the best way for me to get the job done, and it worked well enough for our team to win three Super Bowls.

If you are a business executive, you have to find the approach that works for you. There's more than one way to attack any job. But the one thing all winning programs have in common is solid preparation.

I didn't know any other way to do my job and still be successful. There were times — the 1989 season, for example — when I backed off. I shortened practice and cut the hours we spent in meetings. I thought it might refresh everyone.

The result was that our team became sloppy. We won only five of our first eleven games in 1989. I went back to long meetings and tough practices, and we won our last five games to finish with a 10–6 record.

Every time I backed off an inch, the team backed off an inch, too. I decided to keep doing things the old-fashioned way. To get the absolute most out of the team, the hard way was the way to go.

With the Redskins, our offensive coaches worked the longest hours. I put a lot of faith in my coaching staff, which could be compared to an executive committee in business. I had some of the best assistant coaches in the game, and I really leaned on those guys.

We spent long hours together in the meeting room. It was a small room with no windows. We called it "the submarine" because that was what it felt like in there some nights when we worked until 2:00 A.M. with no contact with the outside world.

We prepared our game plan as a staff. We went through the whole package: first-down plays, goal-line series, third-and-short, third-and-long. We went over the whole plan, piece by piece.

There were six coaches in the room, including me. Each guy voiced his opinion. If I suggested a play that our line coach Jim Hanifan didn't like, he would say, "Wait a minute, that won't work," and explain why. Another coach would then chime in, and so on.

They were very knowledgeable football men. If an idea was mulled over and approved by that group, it had to be a good idea. From that standpoint, it was an excellent system.

The disadvantage was the time factor. To take each play and discuss it took hours. Not every person is capable of working that way. I was lucky because I didn't lose many coaches over the years. When I did lose one, I had to be careful in hiring a replacement. I made sure he understood the demands. If a coach wasn't a night person, he wasn't cut out for our staff.

Other coaches operated differently. For example, I heard that Tom Landry in Dallas segmented work among his assistants, and then they took the work home. The line coach would take one part of the game plan, the receivers coach would take another part, and so on.

When they came back the next day, they put it together with Tom in charge, saying, "I like this. We'll use this. No, I don't like that." It was an interesting way to do things, and it allowed the staff to get home most nights in time for dinner.

Clearly, it worked for the Cowboys because they were a superbly coached team. Their running game was among the best every year, even though it was not very physical. They utilized trap plays and misdirection runs, more finesse than power. The Cowboys did that kind of thing better than anyone else.

Still, I preferred doing things my way, putting a game plan together from scratch, with the whole staff contributing. It was demanding; but every time I talked about changing or cutting back, the other coaches would say, "Don't do it. This works for us."

I work the same way today with my racing team. I have a strong executive committee with my sons, J. D. and Coy; our marketing director, Dave Alpern; and our financial advisors, Don and Todd Meredith. We talk over every major decision. I want to hear what they have to say. I may start out thinking one way, but then have those guys turn me in a completely different direction.

Don came to me after one meeting and said, "This is the way you coached, too, right? Now I see what you're doing."

I hadn't thought of it in those terms, but he was right. The more information you put on the table, whether it is preparing for a Super Bowl, a Daytona 500, or a company expansion, the better your chances of making the right decision.

With the Redskins, our defensive staff operated separately. I had a great defensive coach in Richie Petitbon, and I let him run the show. I sat in on his Tuesday meeting just to see what he was doing, but I seldom said anything more than "Keep up the good work."

Richie was a morning guy. He preferred to get his staff in bright and early. The coaches would do their planning, meet with the players, practice, meet again, and take off. The defensive staff did not spend its nights locked in the submarine.

No defensive coach will admit it, but it takes longer to prepare an offense. Now that I'm out of football, I can say so. With defense, it is a matter of setting a plan and reacting to what happens on the field. It is far more complicated on offense. You have so many details: blocking schemes, pass protection, blitz pickups, pass patterns, reads, adjustments, and on and on.

There are two approaches to offensive preparation. Either you can prepare to do whatever it is that you do best, or you focus on exploiting a weak spot in your opponent's defense. The ideal preparation includes both ways, taking what you do best and matching it to a flaw in the opposition.

An example of the success we had with that approach was when we played Philadelphia in the late 1980s. The Eagles had one of the league's best defenses under coach Buddy Ryan. They were extremely aggressive, blitzing on almost every down. They would send all four linemen, usually one or two linebackers, and possibly a safety after the quarterback.

The Eagles generated tremendous pressure on the passer, but they committed so many players to the rush that it left their secondary vulnerable. When we played them, we matched our offensive line, which was one of our strengths, against their rush, and counted on our wide receivers to beat their defensive backs, one-on-one.

The key was our pass protection. If we gave our quarterback time to deliver the ball, we knew our receivers would be open for big plays. One of our most satisfying games was a 20–6 victory over the Eagles in a 1990 NFC Divisional Play-off Game. We were underdogs; but our line kept the rush off quarterback Mark Rypien, and he threw two touchdown passes to win the game.

We had excellent receivers, and I always looked for new ways to utilize them. One trick was the Bunch package. We put three receivers together, bunched them on one side, and sent them scattering at the snap of the ball. One would break deep, one would break right, and the other left. It was like fireworks — we had receivers going in every direction. We unveiled the offense against the Cowboys, and they didn't know what hit them.

Pro football, like business, is evolving all the time. With the Redskins, we changed about 30 percent of what we did every year. That was typical of most teams. That means if you stood still for one season, you fell behind by 30 percent.

I have a friend in Los Angeles who runs a company. He had matchbooks made up with a picture of a dinosaur and the message: "Adapt or die." That is a good assessment of modern business. You have to stay on top of what's going on, or the game is over for you.

I see it all the time in the NFL. Someone will come up with a new concept, and it will knock the whole league for a loop. There was a four-man defensive front, then a three-man line, then the Buddy Ryan "46," which resembled a seven-man front. Each new look had offenses scrambling.

But the longer a team stays with a particular idea, the more likely it is that the rest of the league will catch up. You have to be changing constantly. You even might borrow an old idea from somewhere else and make it your own.

With the Redskins, we borrowed the "counter-gap," which became our signature play in the 1980s. We were in a staff meeting and Don Breaux, one of the coaches, said, "I just saw a college game on TV, and Nebraska has a running play that's killing everybody."

He diagrammed it on the board, and right away we knew it was a perfect fit for our offense.

On the play, one side of the offensive line pulls as if the play were a sweep around end. That gets the defensive line and linebackers moving away. Then our guard and tackle from the other side would come blasting right through the middle, followed by the ball carrier.

The play requires offensive linemen who can move and running backs who can explode through a hole. We had athletes who possessed those skills. As a result, we had great success with the counter-gap.

In Super Bowl XXII we started a rookie halfback, Timmy Smith, who gained 204 yards running that same play over and over. The Denver defense, with its small linemen and linebackers, could not cope with it. We won easily, 42–10.

Once you establish a play like that, your opponents study it and prepare for it. That preoccupation also can be used to your advantage by making the defense think you are running that play when you actually are doing something else.

We put in a pass play off the counter-gap that was devastating. It was the best play-action pass I've ever seen. We executed the play as though it were a run, but the quarterback faked a handoff and threw a deep pass. The first few times we ran it, the receiver was a full twenty yards behind everyone for a touchdown reception.

Of course, defenses caught up with it. They caught up with the counter-gap, too, because as more teams copied it, defenses became quicker to recognize it. That's one of the things I love about football. It never stands still.

Sell Your Belief

I talk a great deal about the importance of a game plan and the hours of work that go into it. But as head coach, you do not end your work there.

Once you have the plan, you must sell it to the players. It

is not enough to put it on the blackboard and say, "Okay, here it is." You have to convince the players that the plan is a good one and show them, in specific ways, why it will work. If you do, you send them out to the practice field with more confidence.

It was easy for me because I spent so much time on the game plan that, by the time I finished it, I really believed in it. I knew it would work. When I presented it to the team on Wednesday, I displayed my confidence — and the players picked up on it.

It works the same way in any business. You first must believe in your product or service. You know what you've got out there in the marketplace or on the drawing board. You helped create it. You know everything about it. It is your job to sell not only your product but your belief in it.

If you present an idea by saying, "I think this will work," or "This might have a chance," you lose the group. How can you convince anyone to buy into your idea when you aren't convinced yourself?

Once you have sold the game plan, you can begin to teach it. We started with all the players in one room and went over the whole plan. Then we broke into groups with the various coaches taking their units and reviewing their responsibilities.

After meetings we went out on the field and reversed the process. We did individual drills first, then unit work. Finally the whole team worked together. So in the classroom, we started with the big picture and worked down to the individual level. On the practice field, we started with the individual and built up to encompass the team.

This system allowed everyone to grasp what was going on. As a head coach or manager, you must keep in mind that not everyone learns the same way. What may reach one player may not reach another. So you can't teach one way and expect everyone to learn at the same rate. It won't happen.

Some players learn just by listening. Tell them what to do and they do it. Others learn a play by seeing it on the blackboard or on film. Still others need to get on the field and actually run through it.

I could see the comprehension level in their eyes. Some guys would come out of a meeting and have the game plan down cold. They would go on the field and know exactly what to do. I could see other guys trying to take what they saw on the blackboard and adapt it to the field. Once they grasped it, they were fine.

We taught our game plan in such a way that the players heard it, saw it, and then performed it. It was a three-step process, which made it accessible to everyone.

We also filmed our practices so that if a player was making a mistake in a particular pattern or coverage, we could see it and correct it before it hurt us in a game. A player learns fastest that way, watching himself on tape while a coach points out what he is doing wrong.

I demanded a lot from our players, but no more than I demanded from myself. If the top executive works as hard as or harder than everyone else, then it is easy for him to manage the group. He is not just telling people to do things, he is living it, too.

As hard as I pushed our guys at times, I never felt guilty about it — because I was working right along with them. That is management by example. It works a lot better than trying to find some artificial method to motivate your staff. I couldn't say, "You fellows stay late, I'm going home," and then try to justify it.

Set Goals, Reward Achievement

There are two areas in which I feel football does a much better job of management than the typical business: defining goals and rewarding achievement.

In business a company may go months without any clear-cut goals. People who work at those companies show up every day, put in their hours, and go home without any sense of whether they won or lost. Even good workers lose their focus in that kind of environment.

Football takes care of that problem by sending out a schedule and putting scoreboards in the stadiums. As a coach, I knew exactly what my goal was every week. One week it was to defeat the Dallas Cowboys. The next week it was to beat the Miami Dolphins. Every week there was another team.

In business it gets awfully confusing. There are too many people who cannot articulate their goals.

Take a worker in a corporation that fails to turn a profit. As a consequence, he receives no bonuses. Pretty soon, that worker has busted his butt for six months but can't tell you why. His job has become a menial chore. That is how you douse the competitive fire in an individual.

Smart businesses avoid this pitfall by setting goals. If you are in sales, establish a quota for your staff to meet. If you are in the service field, have your customers rate your service one through ten — and set a goal for your staff.

Unless you have a quantitative way of measuring performance, you are operating in a vacuum. You cannot compete that way.

I thought nothing could be more competitive than pro football. But since making the move to auto racing, I've found the business world is just as ferocious. I adapted many of the techniques I used as a coach to running my racing company. Competition and goal-setting are a big part of my approach.

Our racing team has three profit centers: sponsorship, souvenir sales, and winnings. We always are trying to make money and, when possible, save money. We set goals for the three centers, let workers in those areas compete, and reward the ones who produce the best results. The better the competition, the better it is for the company.

Even the top guy, the CEO, needs to quantify his position. He needs a clear understanding of the nature of his job. Before an executive takes a CEO post with a company, he should ask, "What are my goals? What do you expect from me? What does the board want?"

Be specific. Get it on the table.

Before I took a CEO job, I would make sure there was a scoreboard in the office. If there wasn't one, I would create one real fast. I'd say, "Your company did a billion dollars in business last year. What are you looking for this year? A billion and a half?"

If that was an acceptable goal, and I felt it was reachable, then we would have something to work toward. The line between a winning season and a bad season has been defined.

I never liked being in a position where I was judged subjectively. One of the things I don't like about television — I've worked as a pro football analyst on NBC the past few years — is that it places me in such a position. A network executive can say, "That guy has a high-pitched voice and I don't like his hair. Get rid of him."

I don't have any control in that situation.

At least in pro football, tough as it was, I had a win-loss record to make my case. The team owner could have fired me at any time, true. But it probably wasn't going to happen as long as we kept winning. I knew that, and so did everyone else.

As a coach, I was a big believer in rewarding achievement. If you set goals, which we did, you have to reward the people who reach those goals. Give them something extra.

With the Redskins when we won a game, we gave a portable TV to the outstanding player. We also gave clothes and free dinners to players who reached specific goals, whether they were special-teams tackles or quarterback sacks.

In my first season as head coach, we lost our first five games. I had nightmares about being the only coach in NFL history to go winless in his career. We broke the streak with a 24–7 victory over Chicago. I was so elated, I gave away five TVs instead of just one.

We did other things to reward the players, such as treating them to barbecued ribs and ice cream after practice. That was a midweek bonus after a real good victory. The players got so excited that they looked like kids at a birthday party.

Another thing about rewards — select them with care because you may have to pay off.

I learned my lesson in 1987 when I promised to let Alvin Walton, one of our safeties, cut my hair if we won the Super Bowl. Alvin was one of the first players to shave his head, so the joke was he could do the same to me if we won the NFL championship.

I don't know if the idea of seeing me bald inspired the team or what. But we played great down the stretch and dominated Denver in the Super Bowl. I thought that maybe in all the excitement, the players might forget our deal. No chance.

Five months later, when we held our minicamp, the players called for the haircut. I asked for a delay until training camp. The players said no.

I promised to give them an extra day off during camp if they forgot the whole thing. I thought surely they would jump at that offer. They said no way.

So I submitted.

The funny thing was Alvin, the designated barber, was so nervous that he couldn't stop his hands from shaking. He handed the scissors to Mark May, our offensive guard, who gave me the flattest flattop you ever saw.

There probably are a few photos of me in that haircut still floating around. If you need a good laugh — or a scare! — check them out. But I had made a deal and stuck to it. That also is part of good management.

In football, business, and life, I find that honesty is the best motivator. If the people who work for you believe what you say, they will respond.

Be honest in setting goals for your team. Be honest about the task ahead, even if it means telling the players, "This is going to be rough." I don't believe in playing mind games. That only confuses matters.

I'll give you an example. One of the toughest assignments in pro football is getting ready to play the week after a Monday night game. For the players, the short week means less time for injuries to heal. For the coaches, it means less time to prepare for the next opponent.

You might think our Redskins team, with its emphasis on extensive preparation, would be hurt more than other clubs by a short week. But we actually did very well in those situations.

Our Redskins teams had twenty-one games when we played on Sunday following a Monday night game, and our record was 19–2. Ten of the Monday games were on the road, which made matters worse, because we did not return to Washington until the wee hours of Tuesday morning.

Typically the whole team was drained not only by the trip but by the game itself, because Monday night games tend to be very intense and hard-hitting. So how did our coaches and players bounce back?

I believe honesty was the key. I was honest with the coaches and players. I'd say, "It's going to be brutal around here the next few days. But if we can get through Tuesday night and put together a game plan, and then put it on the field Wednesday, we're back on schedule. So let's suck it up and do it."

I promised the players a reward. If they practiced well, I gave them a break during the next morning meeting; we had muffins, coffee, and juice brought in. We might have pizza after practice another day. Those were small things, but they helped keep everyone going.

You are better off when you tell people up front that something is going to be hard. The worst thing you can do as a head coach is say, "Today will be an easy practice." Once you say that, the players gear themselves to do nothing. You might as well not practice at all.

Tell the players it is going to be rough; they might not like it, but at least they're mentally ready for it.

Some coaches and teams look for excuses to lose. Coming off a Monday night game is one example. If a coach dwells on what a disadvantage it is, the players hear that and think, "We're not supposed to win the next game."

I never gave my teams an excuse to fail. Even when we

went through tough times, I didn't say, "Our defense is too slow" or "Our quarterback is too young." Players hear that and think, "We're not good enough to win."

My general response after a loss was, "We didn't get it done today" or "The other team outplayed us." I made it clear that we were capable of playing better. It is important that you give your people something on which to build.

Meet Adversity Head On

Adversity is a part of any business. I had my share of it when I was coaching the Redskins, although our successes outweighed our problems. When adversity hits, don't waste time crying about it. Meet it head on.

There were times when I took situations that other people considered traumatic and turned them to our advantage. Good examples are the two seasons that were interrupted by player strikes, 1982 and 1987.

Our team won the Super Bowl in each of the strike seasons. We were able to win at a time when other teams were coming apart at the seams. In a sense, we took advantage of a bad situation.

How? By not giving in to it.

Whenever a business or sport hits a traumatic period or sudden downturn, it is a given that some companies or teams will not handle it well. If your company can just keep it together, you will have an advantage over the competition.

Don't think of trouble as a negative, but seize it as an opportunity to lap the field. Some NFL teams used the strike as an excuse to write off the season. It was disruptive, it was distracting, and so on. We agreed it wasn't ideal, but we still had our jobs to do.

In 1982 the players went on strike after the second regular-season game and stayed out for two months. They came back in November, and we finished the year with an expanded post-season playoff tournament. In all, our team played thirteen games and won twelve, including a 27–17 victory over Miami in Super Bowl XVII.

How did we succeed in coping with the strike? We kept our wits about us as an organization. As coaches, we did not get drawn into the battle between the players and management. We did not comment on the strike because we did not want to leave scars on either side.

When the strike was settled and the players returned, our approach was business as usual. I didn't rip the players for their actions. I made it clear that no one in the organization held any grudges.

I knew the players were not happy. They felt they did not have much to show for their strike. I said, "Look, you took your best shot. That's over with now. Are you going to worry about that, or are you going to try to win the Super Bowl and make some money back for yourselves?"

We put the strike behind us and moved on. Our first game back we beat the Giants, 27–17. We rolled on from there.

The 1987 strike was an even touchier situation. When the players went on strike that time, the league decided to continue playing games with replacement players. Each club had to scramble to assemble a team of replacement players, then whip them into shape in two weeks.

As coaches, we were caught in the middle, working with a team of replacements while our real players walked a picket line. Again, we decided to make the best of a bad situation.

General manager Charley Casserly, who then was Bobby Beathard's assistant, did a good job assembling our replacement team. As a group, it probably was the most talented of the twenty-eight replacement teams. Our coaches did the best job they could preparing them to play. The result was that we won all three replacement games, and those three victories really helped us on the way to Super Bowl XXII.

Some clubs did not take the replacement teams as seriously as we did, perhaps because they did not expect the strike to last. As a result, they were stuck with teams that were not competitive and wound up losing valuable games. By staying with our business-as-usual approach, we gained ground.

We were helped by the fact that our striking players stuck together. I made that appeal to our guys when the decision was made to play replacement games. A number of veterans on other teams crossed the picket line and played in the replacement games. I didn't want that, because I didn't want any splits in our squad.

I told our striking players, "We'll be back together someday, and I don't want a team that's divided. Stick together, work out together, and keep in shape. Meanwhile, we'll try to win as many games as we can with this replacement team."

We came through the strike in good shape, but some other clubs that had a large number of veterans cross the picket line had trouble with morale after the strike.

Free agency is another case in which some clubs are knocked for a loop, while others know how to handle it. A smart team will lock up its top six or seven players with long-term contracts. That will ensure stability. Other teams will scramble around without a plan, then blame the system when they lose.

In football and life, you should be learning all the time. If you're not, you just aren't paying attention. As a result, you are not going to go very far.

When I look back on our 1982 Super Bowl season, I realize that it began to take shape during the 0–5 start the previous year. The low point of my coaching career actually set the stage for our first NFL championship.

We learned a lot about ourselves as a team in that five-game losing streak. It opened my eyes to some personnel changes that had to be made. Also, while looking for a way to improve our offense, we hit upon the one-back set. That became our bread-and-butter formation.

Going through that losing streak in 1981 left me with a burning desire never to pass that way again. I never forgot the way I felt that first season. The coaches who were there also remembered it. That experience was *always* in the back of our minds. You'd better believe it pushed us.

I kept a few mementos from the 1981 season. One of them was a sports section from a Washington newspaper dated October 5, the day after we lost to San Francisco, 30–17, to drop to 0–5. I kept that newspaper in my office until I resigned. I didn't ever want to forget what those days were like.

I also kept a videotape of what the local sportscasters said about me when we were 0–5: "Who is this guy? Joe who? He can't win a game."

Every time I got to thinking, "Hey, Joe, you're a pretty good coach; everybody loves you," I popped that tape in the VCR, and it brought me back down to earth.

It was funny to see those TV guys and what they were saying about me then and compare it with what they said about me later. It makes you realize it's a real short trip from the top to the bottom, and you never should lose track of where you are.

When we were struggling in 1981, I don't think any of us could have guessed that a Super Bowl was right around the corner. Our leap from 8–8 in 1981 to NFL champions the next season was a stunner, even to me.

The 1982 team wasn't the most talented team we ever had, but we had one player who lifted our entire club to another level. That was John Riggins, our fullback.

When I was hired in Washington, Riggins was out of football. He had left the Redskins' camp in 1980 after the team refused to renegotiate his contract. A free spirit, John announced his retirement and sat out the season on his farm in Kansas.

As a rookie head coach, I wanted to coax Riggins back. I flew to Lawrence, Kansas, drove to the first gas station I saw, and got directions to John's farm. I turned onto a dirt road, and drove until I saw the house. John's wife, Mary Lou, answered the door.

I introduced myself as the new head coach of the Redskins. I said I wanted John to play for us. Mary Lou said, "I think that would be a good idea." At that point, I knew I had a chance.

John was away hunting, but Mary Lou suggested I check into the local motel. The next morning, she called to say John would meet me at the house at 10:00 A.M.

When I arrived, John was waiting outside, still in his hunting clothes. Halfway through breakfast, John looked me in the eye and said, "I'll tell you something. If you get me back there, I'll make you famous."

I flew back to Washington, still not sure what to make of the guy. A few days later, he called to say he was coming back. I was pleased but really didn't know what to expect. He was thirty-one years old. Could he still do the job?

Little did I realize that two years later, Riggins would carry our team to the NFL title. In four postseason games, Riggins rushed for 610 yards. In Super Bowl XVII, against Miami, he carried the ball thirty-eight times for 166 yards, broke the game open with a 43-yard touchdown run in the fourth quarter, and was named the game's MVP.

In the process, Riggins made good on his promise: He made me famous.

The moral of the story is that it's your job, as a boss, to find people who are productive — even if it means flying to Kansas and interviewing a guy in a camouflage outfit.

There wasn't one time that Riggins asked for the ball when he didn't produce. If you want to be successful, surround yourself with the right kind of people. Because the best game plan in the world is worthless if the coaches aren't capable of teaching it or the players aren't capable of absorbing it.

I believe that picking the right people is the single most important thing a coach or boss can do. If you pick sharp, highly motivated people, you're going to be successful.

As much time and effort as I put into the Xs and Os of business, I think that it is the people around you who really make the difference. In Washington I had a group of assistant coaches who were willing to work sixteen hours a day, and I had a bunch of players who accepted every challenge put in front of them.

Picking the right people doesn't mean going back to the

same mold all the time. It isn't a matter of style. It is a matter of results. That a person is productive and a hard worker is all that matters. Riggins certainly didn't fit any mold, but he helped us win a championship.

I have the distinction of being the only head coach to win three Super Bowls with three different starting quarterbacks. They were, in order, Joe Theismann, Doug Williams, and Mark Rypien. They all were different in what they were able to do, but each was a winner. Doug and Mark were selected as the most valuable players in their two victories.

Theismann was a fiery guy, adept at moving around, rolling out, and throwing on the run. Williams was a veteran who had a strong arm but not much mobility. Rypien was the youngest of the three and the most unassuming. Mark never said much; he just did his job.

They were different guys with different strengths, but what they had in common was intelligence, toughness, and a will to win. I did not have to change the offense very much when we changed quarterbacks. All three could execute our system. I had complete confidence in each of them.

The Price of Intensity

When I was a college assistant, I set a goal for myself. I wanted to be a head coach either at the college level or in the pros by the time I was thirty-four. That time passed, and I had only one interview — at the University of Arizona — and didn't get the job. I started to think I was a failure.

But the Lord blessed me with the opportunity to move up to the NFL as an assistant under Don Coryell in St. Louis. When Don went to San Diego, he brought me along as offensive coordinator. I worked with a pair of future Hall of Famers there — quarterback Dan Fouts and tight end Kellen Winslow — and we set an NFL record for passing yardage in 1980.

That success brought me to the attention of Jack Kent

Cooke, the owner of the Redskins. He hired me as head coach the following season.

On the field in Washington, I had twelve great years. We made the playoffs in eight of those seasons and went to four Super Bowls. But I had a huge setback off the field in 1984 when a land deal I had invested in went sour.

I became involved in the deal shortly after we won our first Super Bowl. An old college friend was a builder. He had a plan to put up a bunch of homes and apartment complexes. He was looking for investors and called me. I said I was interested, although I hardly qualified as a businessman.

My friend assured me these properties would rent quickly and pay for themselves in no time. I visited the first site and was so impressed that I invested in fourteen homes in one day. I invested in others over time.

I felt I was doing a wise thing: securing my family's future and putting myself in a position so that if someday I felt like walking away from football, I'd still have a nice source of income. My motives were good, but my judgment was lousy.

Things seemed to go well at first, but in the second year I started getting late notices. The mortgages on some of the houses I had signed for weren't being paid. I thought it was an accounting error. But the notices kept coming.

I called my friend, who admitted some of the units weren't moving as quickly as he had hoped. Time passed, and the problems mounted. Because my name was on the papers, creditors came looking for me.

I asked Todd Meredith, my business advisor, to assess the situation. I had no idea how bad things were. Todd found there were nine banks involved and I was more than a million dollars in debt. The interest alone was $30,000 a month. I was bankrupt.

It was shattering news, but I had only myself to blame. I totally ignored the cardinal rule I followed as a coach: Be prepared; attend to every detail. I invested my money and trusted someone else to make the right calls. I was too busy with football to stay on top of the situation.

I was in over my head but didn't realize it until it was too late. I was lucky, because with Todd's help, I worked out a deal with the banks that paid off the debt and took the properties off my hands. I learned a valuable lesson: Never leave things unattended. I'm a much smarter businessman today.

That was a case where my single-minded dedication to football got me in trouble. But as I mentioned earlier, I did not know another way to coach. I worked at it, literally, around the clock. It took its toll on me, I knew that.

The longer the season went, the wearier I felt. Before some games, after I rewrote the game plan for the umpteenth time, I would stretch out on the locker room floor and sleep for twenty minutes. Friends urged me to slow down; but every time I tried to, I felt like I was short-changing the team.

I became so absorbed in my job as Redskins head coach that I lost touch with the world outside my submarine. When the press was finished asking me questions about our football team, I would ask the reporters questions about what was happening in the world. I didn't know about Oliver North, one of the figures in the Iran-Contra scandal, until he visited one of our practices.

One Thursday evening, I was leaving to tape my weekly TV show and couldn't find my car in the parking lot. I was about to report it stolen when I remembered I had left it at a nearby hotel before the previous road game.

One of the other coaches drove me to the hotel, but there was another problem: I couldn't remember where I left the keys. I was running late, so I borrowed the other coach's car to drive into town. He had to call the office so someone could come over and pick him up.

There are dozens of similar stories about me, and they all reflect a coach consumed by his work. Finally in March 1993 I decided I had had enough. I resigned, saying I wanted to try a different life for a while.

There were a number of factors. My health was one. I was getting headaches and feeling run-down. The doctors diagnosed it as migraine equivalence. It wasn't serious but, combined with my age, fifty-two, and my being forty pounds over-weight, it was enough to give me pause.

I wanted to spend more time with Pat and our two sons. The 1992 season had been a tough one because our family was separated — J. D. was working full-time at our racing office in Charlotte and Coy was attending Stanford.

It was very hard for Pat, who was left alone many nights because of my work routine and the boys being so far away. In addition, I had reached a point in coaching in which the pressure outweighed the fun. When you're in that position for a while, you find the victories don't mean as much and the losses hurt more. People take winning for granted, but they still ask, "Why?" when you lose. It wears on you.

Walking away from football was tough. I had spent my whole life in football and twenty-eight years coaching it. It was the one area where I qualified as an expert. To leave it was a scary proposition.

The easy thing would have been to stay on. The Redskins are a great organization. Mr. Cooke is a great owner. And I had the best coaching staff in the business. I could have sucked it up and kept going, but I didn't feel that it was the right thing to do. My heart wasn't in it anymore, and it would have shown.

Once I made the decision, I never looked back. I thought I might have second thoughts when Super Bowl time came around and I saw other coaches there. That didn't happen.

I don't miss the NFL competition because I have competition on the NASCAR circuit. The only difference is I'm the owner; and the crew chief, Jimmy Makar, acts as the head coach. He makes the calls on race day. I'm there, but I don't get involved in the strategy.

All those years in Washington, I never understood how Mr. Cooke got such a kick out of being an owner. Now I'm in that position and appreciate it more. The team is your baby, and when it wins the big one — whether it's the Super Bowl or Daytona 500 — it's a thrill. The thrill of winning is always big.

Hands-On Management

Mike Ditka

HEAD COACH

CHICAGO BEARS, 1982—92

Mike Ditka coached the game of football the same way he played it — with a fierce determination that bordered on rage. He had no use for losing or for those who would accept it.

Pro Football Hall of Fame running back Gale Sayers recalls Ditka as a teammate on the Chicago Bears in the 1960s. "Mike would scream at other players in practice," Sayers says. "He was such an intense competitor. He hated anyone who gave less than a hundred-percent effort."

Ditka's personality reflects his roots in Aliquippa, a blue-collar corner of western Pennsylvania, where his father, an ex-Marine, worked for the railroad.

"There was a certain way you had to live, certain things you were expected to do there," Ditka says. "There was no 'maybe.' There was no doing anything *halfway* right. You did something *all the way* right."

Ditka began his football career as a defensive end at Aliquippa High School. He developed into an All-America end and linebacker at Pitt.

Drafted by the Bears in 1961, the six-foot three-inch, 225-pound Ditka played twelve seasons in the NFL and caught 427 passes, which stood as the record for tight ends for two decades.

He was also a punishing blocker, one of the best ever at his position. In 1988 Ditka was inducted into the Pro Football Hall of Fame.

Looking back on his career, Ditka once said, "All I know is I played hard. I didn't make many friends. I respect players who play the game that way. I'm not saying it's the only way you can play it, but it's not a bad way."

After Ditka's retirement as a player, he worked for nine years as an assistant coach under Tom Landry in Dallas. Then in 1982 team owner George Halas brought him back to Chicago as head coach of the Bears.

Only forty-two, with no head-coaching experience, Ditka seemed like a risky choice, but Halas knew exactly what he was doing. The Bears had lost their identity, their trademark toughness. Halas felt if anyone could put the team back on top, it was the man known as Iron Mike.

As Ray Sons wrote in the *Chicago Sun-Times:* "Ditka is the keeper of their flame, a throwback to George Halas. He is the Bears. The Bears are Ditka."

In eleven seasons as Chicago's head coach, Ditka led the Bears to a 112–68 record. He took the team from the bottom of the NFC to a Super Bowl championship in four years. The Bears made the playoffs seven times under Ditka; he twice was named NFL Coach of the Year.

Ditka, who has had both hips replaced as a result of football injuries, limped up and down the sidelines at Soldier Field, sometimes berating, other times encouraging, but almost always inspiring his Bears with a coaching style that reflected the brawny swagger of Chicago itself.

Ditka once referred to his team as "a bunch of Grabowskis," meaning a collection of tough-minded, hard-nosed working stiffs of which he was both boss and father figure.

"He gives off an aura," tight end Brent Novoselsky once said. "You know when he's in the room. His stare — you're really aware of it. You realize he is watching at all times."

In November 1988 Ditka suffered a mild heart attack. He was back on the sidelines eleven days later, watching his Bears defeat

Washington, 34–14. His cardiologist advised him against returning so soon, but Ditka was not about to listen. Instead, the doctor simply walked the sidelines in Washington with him.

"It's his job to advise me to take it slow," Ditka said afterward. "But it's my job to coach. On game day, I'm here."

E very time I hear people talk about "coaching philosophy," I have to smile. I was involved in football, as a player and a coach, for forty years and never had a philosophy other than "whip the other guy."

People sometimes make the game more complicated than it is. They make the business of coaching seem complex, too, when in fact I think it is pretty simple. You get good athletes who want to win, give them a system that maximizes their strengths, and then work at it.

It isn't profound, but that is how I coached for nine years as an assistant coach with Dallas and for eleven seasons as head coach in Chicago.

In 1982 when George Halas interviewed me for the job in Chicago, he asked about my offensive and defensive philosophies. I still remember it. We were sitting at his kitchen table, and he was staring at me very intently, the same way he did when I played for him as a crew-cut tight end.

I said, "Coach, you didn't bring me here to talk about philosophy. I have one philosophy and it's the same as yours — to kick the other guy's ass. That's why you brought me here and you know it.

"If you want to hire me, we should talk about that and cut out this other crap because we're only wasting time."

Mr. Halas smiled, and that was it. I had the job, the only job I ever really wanted — head coach of the Chicago Bears.

I broke into the National Football League with the Bears in 1961 and played six seasons in Chicago. I played six more years in Philadelphia and Dallas. I won a Super Bowl ring with the Cowboys in 1972. But at heart, I was always a Chicago Bear.

Tom Landry, the head coach in Dallas, knew that. He kept me on his coaching staff after I retired as a player in 1973. We often disagreed in staff meetings. Tom would say, "Mike, you're a Bear; you're too basic."

I just felt the basics, done well, are what win football games. I still believe that. And that belief also applies to other areas of life.

It is very important for the head of any organization, whether it is a football team, a major corporation, or a corner store, to have a clear idea of what his business stands for. If you cannot define what it is you want to be, then you're not going to be much of anything.

How many successful people have you ever heard say, "I just make it up as I go along?" I can't think of one.

I had a very definite idea of how I wanted people to perceive the Bears. I wanted them to think we were the roughest, toughest SOBs who ever lived. We had that identity in the 1960s when I played in Chicago, but the team lost its bite in the 1970s.

Playing against the Bears and coaching against them while I was in Dallas, I could see the team lacked discipline. The players made fundamental mistakes. They dropped their heads when they fell behind. They looked like losers. In most cases, they played like losers.

That attitude was the first thing I had to address when I took over as head coach. If I was going to rebuild the Bears, I had to start at the beginning. I had to spell out what it meant to be a Bear and determine which players had the stuff and which ones did not.

It meant being very clear about my goals right from Day One. I was only forty-two years old and had never been a head coach before, so there were a lot of skeptics in the media and on the team who were ready to laugh me out of town.

I knew it but couldn't let it affect the way I approached the job.

At the first team meeting, I stood in front of the room with my arms folded. Once all the players were in their seats, I nodded to assistant coach Ted Plumb and he began calling roll. Hall of Fame running back Walter Payton later said the first thing that crossed his mind was, "Uh-oh, we're in the Army now."

Some players sat up a little straighter in their chairs. Others shot looks to their buddies or rolled their eyes.

I didn't say anything, but I took mental notes. It was a test. Some guys passed; others flunked.

Then I gave my talk. I said the Chicago Bears were going to win the Super Bowl. I said that was my goal, that was why Mr. Halas hired me, and that was what we were going to do.

I believed it: I wanted to see how many of the players believed it. The ones who smirked and nudged each other — and there were a few — were gone. I got rid of those eggheads as quickly as I could.

But I saw excitement in the faces of players like Payton, Mike Singletary, Gary Fencik, and Doug Plank. I knew I could build around those guys because they wanted the same thing I wanted: to win the whole thing.

I held up my Super Bowl ring and asked, "Is this what's important? Yes or no? Or is it the paycheck that's important?" I said there are a lot of places in the world to pick up a paycheck. I didn't want any player who was in it just for that. I wanted players who would work for the team.

Just so they didn't think I was blowing smoke, I broke it down for them. I reviewed what the offense and defense had done the previous season and compared it with teams that made the playoffs. In most cases, we weren't that far behind. It was a few yards here and there, a matter of two or three plays a game.

I said, "Here's the difference, guys. This is what you have to make up. Is that impossible?"

When it was presented that way, they got the message.

For years they had heard nothing but negatives. Every time they turned around or picked up a newspaper, someone was telling them they stunk. I went the opposite way. I said, "Hey, fellas, you're this close to being really good."

I knew the good guys would accept that challenge, and they did.

We did not turn it around overnight. We could not turn over the whole team in one year. I still had some deadwood on the roster. Also that was a season shortened to nine games by the players' strike, so I did not get as much accomplished as I would have liked. But even at 3–6, we made a start.

Once we began drafting our own players — Jimbo Covert, Jim McMahon, Wilbur Marshall, Matt Suhey — and added them to the core of hungry veterans, such as Payton and Singletary, we improved in a hurry.

We won ten games in 1984. The next year we were 15–1 and won the Super Bowl. That team, the 1985 Bears, will be talked about as one of the great teams of all time.

We put that team together in four years because we had a plan and stuck with it. We brought in Bears-type players and played Bears-style football. We did not feature any one individual, even though we had some great ones, such as Payton. We played as a team, forty men with a common purpose.

A lot was written and said about me being a great motivator. I don't really believe I am.

I think motivation is the most overused, overrated, overplayed word in our society. I don't believe there is such a thing as motivation, at least not in the sense that most people use the word to describe pep talks and backslapping and all that stuff. Motivation comes from within each individual. It is a personal thing. It is pride, guts, desire, whatever you want to call it; some people have it in their bellies, and some don't.

If you want to win, you find people who have that quality and put them on your team. In business you find good people who relish the idea of being part of something successful, of helping to build it and see it grow. You recruit them and then run with them.

You must spell out your program, describe what your goals are, what your methods are for reaching those goals, how you expect to attain them. And that's it. In football, we call it a game plan. You *must* have one.

It is like a pyramid. You start with what the main goal is, then you break it down to what the individual goals are. If you get to the point where everyone on the team has the same goal — for us, it was to win the Super Bowl — then you can do it.

But you can't succeed if you have people with a lot of different goals: one guy wants to own a big car, one wants to catch a lot of passes, one wants to get a lot of sacks, and so on. Because that's probably what will happen. One guy *will* get his big car, one guy *will* catch his passes, one guy *will* get his sacks, but you won't win a Super Bowl — because your players have the pyramid upside down. They put individual goals ahead of the team goal.

As a coach, I could give the greatest pregame speech in history, but if the guys in that room aren't already with the program, if they don't want to sacrifice a piece of themselves for the good of the team, I'm not going to change things five minutes before we walk out on the field. That's where the concept of coach-as-motivator falls apart. You can't motivate a guy who won't be motivated. The only thing you can do is get rid of him and bring in someone else.

I've been known to chew out guys on the sidelines and sometimes rip them in the press. In almost every case, the player was someone I felt had a lot to offer and wasn't delivering for some reason.

Defensive tackle William Perry, for instance, is a helluva kid. He did a lot for our team in the Super Bowl year, but he didn't take care of himself. He let his weight get out of control and just couldn't perform anymore. At one time William had the motivation, but then he lost it. That happens, especially in this era of instant fame and million-dollar salaries. It is one of the great challenges of coaching today.

Jim McMahon was another prime example. After our Super Bowl victory, his priorities changed. He rebelled against me, against some of his teammates, but most of all against the organization. He became a deterrent rather than an asset. He had become a disruptive influence, in my opinion, and was hurting the team; so he had to go.

I respect the hell out of McMahon. We would not have won the Super Bowl without him. He was the guy who made it happen. He went on the field and told his teammates to get off their asses, and they responded. He made those offensive linemen better than they were because they became tougher in his presence.

Jim always had a wild streak, which was why some teams shied away from him when he came out of college, but we drafted him because he was a helluva talent. As an organization, you should not be afraid to take a shot on a really talented individual. But a boss has to know how far to go with that individual and when to pull the plug.

I made the decision to trade McMahon during the 1989 preseason. It was obvious he did not want to be a part of the team any longer, so we traded him to San Diego for a future draft choice. I took a lot of criticism for the move, but I wasn't concerned with making people happy. I did what I felt was best for the team.

If I had it to do over again, I'd do the same thing.

Your people must not lose sight of why they are with you, what their roles within your organization are, and how they can contribute. When the distractions of building a résumé, tracking a career path, or monitoring outside investments become more important than everyday performance, I think you have to step in and set valuable employees straight. Or risk losing them, or having to cut them.

Communicate Face-to-Face

I inherited a tough situation when I took over the Bears in 1982. In fact, when I was first rumored to be up for the job, one Chicago columnist wrote: "The way things stand now, next year could be the worst in Bears' history if Ditka comes in."

The problem was a split — actually, several splits — within the organization. Mr. Halas was at odds with Jim

Finks, who was the club's general manager. Finks was supported by Ed McCaskey, the team's vice-president [now chairman of the board] and Mr. Halas's son-in-law. Mr. Halas wanted to hire me as head coach, but Finks wanted to hire George Allen, who previously had coached both the Rams and Redskins.

It was a touchy situation, compounded by the fact that Mr. Halas had retained the defensive coaching staff, headed by defensive coordinator Buddy Ryan. That meant when I took the job, I inherited a group of assistant coaches who had no particular allegiance to, or even liking for, me.

A lot of people, especially those in the media, thought it would be my undoing, that as a rookie head coach I would not be able to pull the pieces together. They were wrong, because I understood the value of one simple word: *communication.*

I communicated well. I communicated with Finks because he was my superior and was calling the shots on personnel. I told him what I felt our needs were, and he went out and got the players. We never had a problem.

I talked to Mr. Halas constantly because I considered him to be my mentor. He was one of the founding fathers of the National Football League; he was in the game his entire adult life as a player, a coach, and an owner. He was someone I could look to for advice in any situation, and I went to him a lot, especially that first year.

I had great respect for Ryan because I knew he was one of the top defensive coordinators in the game. He marched to his own drummer, as they say, but I could live with that as long as he did not stray too far from the team concept. Then I would rein him in.

Ryan would get so immersed in his defense, he would create a situation within the team where it was his guys versus everyone else. I thought it was stupid and told him so.

I'd say, "Look, we don't play the Bears this year. Believe me, they're not on our schedule. So quit trying to impress me with how your guys can kick everyone's ass. Let's worry about getting ready for the people that we really have to play."

That's the kind of situation that can develop in any corporation — one department trying to upstage another, one group working more for itself than the organization as a whole. You, as a manager, have to be aware of that happening with individual employees and stop it before it gets out of control.

Even though Ryan and I had our disagreements, I never tried to take over the defense. I was very much hands-on with the offense and special teams because they were the areas I coached in Dallas, but I delegated the defense to Buddy and left him in charge, although I reserved the right to make suggestions.

Ryan was very shrewd in his own way. He challenged his guys by setting high goals. He would say things like, "We're gonna shut this team out." We could be playing the Canton Bulldogs with Jim Thorpe in his prime; Buddy would say the same thing.

At first I didn't like it, but then I realized what he was doing. He figured the greater the challenge, the harder his guys would play to meet it. When we went into the 1985 post-season, I asked Ryan how he thought we would do. He said, "We'll shut these teams out."

He was right. We beat the Giants, 21–0, and the Rams, 24–0, to reach Super Bowl XX and damn near shut out New England in that game, 46–10.

We allowed one touchdown in three playoff games. I never saw a more dominating defensive performance.

But that was how things worked in our organization. I was in constant contact with everyone, making sure the lines of communication stayed open and serving as a kind of buffer between the various personalities and egos.

I had a rule: Never send a memo. It is the worst thing you can do.

If you need something done, walk down the hall and either do it yourself or tell someone else to do it so you are sure it gets done. Don't put on paper what you can tell someone face-to-face.

You get these people who want to send a memo on everything. All they do is waste paper and waste time. It's so damn inefficient.

Personal contact is part of hands-on management. Go to the other guy's office; tell him what you have in mind so there is no misunderstanding. How many times have you heard someone say, "Oh, *that's* what you wanted"? Get it right from the beginning. You cannot recover wasted time.

Working under Coach Landry in Dallas, first as a player, later as an assistant coach, was a great education. Almost everything I practiced in terms of time management and organization, I learned from Coach Landry.

Tom was the total authority there. He ran everything in the football operation, including personnel. Every part of the game plan went through him: offense, defense, and special teams.

When I became head coach in Chicago, I did not choose to have that kind of broad authority. I was deeply involved in the offense and kicking game, but I let Ryan and his staff handle the defense. When Ryan left, I gave Vince Tobin, his successor, the same kind of autonomy.

Defense wasn't my area, and to get involved just for the sake of getting involved didn't make much sense. I would rather spend my time on the parts of the game that I knew best.

One of the lessons I learned working under Landry was the importance of thinking things through. Dan Reeves, who's now New York Giants head coach, was on the staff, too, and we would think up different formations and plays. We'd go into Tom's office and say, "We just came up with something."

Tom would hear us out and then would say, "Okay, but why is that a good idea?" In other words, Why is that play going to work?

So we would have to draw up the play against whatever defense we were facing that week and show Tom — boom, boom, boom — this is why it will work. We can match up this guy against that guy, block this guy here, send this guy through there, and so on.

It was invaluable because what it taught me was that gut instinct is not enough. Tom was an absolute fanatic on using computer printouts to study the other team's tendencies. We knew how often our opponents passed on first down, how often they ran draw plays on second-and-long, how often they blitzed in the fourth quarter.

Whatever we came up with in terms of plays and formations had to tie in with what the computer told us about the opposition. It made me a more detail-oriented coach instead of a guy who might pull something out of thin air and say, "Let's try this . . ."

In the NFL that kind of coaching usually gets you beat and might get you fired.

In Dallas we had some coaches who occasionally came up with lamebrained ideas and wanted to run triple-reverses and throw passes across the field on kick returns — high-school stuff. Tom would write down the plays and an hour later, you'd see the paper he wrote on in the garbage can.

I believed in everything Tom preached offensively, especially about movement, shifting formations, changing the snap count, and keeping the defense off balance. It is harder to do now with less time between plays, but back then we had enough time to shift, set, and put people in motion. It was a tremendous weapon because it made the defense react — and if they made a mistake, we would take advantage of it.

We always talked about the "what ifs?" What if the other team does this — what do we do? That was how we came up with the spread formation, which was the resurrection of the Shotgun formation that the 49ers used in the early sixties.

It was just some coaches talking. Well, if the defense is going to use five or six backs, why shouldn't we use five or six receivers? Okay, how do we do that? Well, let's put the quarterback deep and spread the receivers so that if the defense blitzes, the receivers can adjust their patterns to get open more quickly.

We talked it out, step by step, until we had studied it from both sides. Finally Tom said, "Let's go with it." Thinking every detail of our game plan through, being thoroughly familiar with our opponents' and our own tendencies, turned out to be a great weapon. Of course, it helped to have quarterback Roger Staubach pulling the trigger.

Execution Before Innovation

You have to be flexible and willing to adjust. But I still believe that execution, not innovation, is what wins games. How well do your guys execute compared with the other guys?

Some coaches stand at a blackboard and diagram plays and look very intellectual, but it means nothing if they can't get the knowledge across to their players or if they can't get their players to believe in the system.

As I stated, the game does not have to be complex. Lombardi proved that. Chuck Noll proved it in Pittsburgh. But it does have to be exacting and does have to be well executed.

When I talk about execution and discipline and how important they are in winning, people sometimes give me a funny look. I know what they're thinking.

"Hey, you coached the 1985 Chicago Bears. McMahon's headbands and sunglasses, the Super Bowl Shuffle, players dressing up like the Blues Brothers. That was *discipline?*"

It was an unusual team, I'll grant you. There were some unique personalities on that ball club, and I know there are some people who would put me in that category, too.

I don't disagree with that.

But I will challenge anyone who said our Super Bowl team was undisciplined because Steve McMichael, our defensive tackle, wore his hair kind of long or because McMahon once dropped his pants at a low-flying TV news helicopter.

That might not pass for discipline in the Marine Corps, but pro football isn't the Marine Corps. And neither is business.

In pro football, as on Wall Street, discipline means showing up on time for meetings, working hard in practice or at your desk, carrying out your assignments, and not committing stupid errors.

In all those areas the 1985 Bears were a very disciplined team; that's how we won eighteen of nineteen games, including Super Bowl XX. The Super Bowl Shuffle video; the marketing blitz that surrounded our players, especially Perry ("the Fridge"); McMahon's running feud with the league office — none of that concerned me because it did not interfere with what we did on the field. If it had, I would have stepped in immediately.

But the 1985 Bears were a bunch of guys with the same purpose. Everyone was pulling for the same cause. We were going to win the Super Bowl; we all felt that. Every person in the organization wanted to be a part of it.

There were times, I know, when it looked as if we had no control over some of the guys — but we did. I didn't have to lean on them very much. They controlled themselves in the sense that they knew, "Hey, we have something special here. Let's not blow it."

For most of the players, the wild-and-crazy image was really a put-on. The whole time they were strutting around in their sunglasses, acting cool, they were really laughing at the media for making such a big deal of it.

The thing was that nobody knew who these guys were before we started to win games. Who knew Steve McMichael? Who knew Dan Hampton? Perry was just a rookie. So when the guys saw the opportunity to create this colorful mystique, they did it. They did a helluva job, too. We were the sports story of the year.

I knew going into the 1985 season that we would be good, but it was the third regular-season game that made me realize we could be something special. We played a Thursday night game in Minnesota, and McMahon was sitting out with a sore neck and bruised leg. Steve Fuller started at quarterback, and we couldn't get anything going, falling behind, 17–9, in the third quarter.

McMahon wanted to play, despite the injuries. I had to make the call: Do I play him and risk further injury? Or do I hold him out, probably lose the game, but make sure he is healthy for the following week?

I could see the fire in Jim's eyes. He really wanted to play. I said, "Okay, go."

His first two passes went for touchdowns, one to Willie Gault for seventy yards, the other to Dennis McKinnon for twenty-five yards. We scored twenty-four points in the quarter and won easily, 33–24.

After that game, I knew. We were on our way.

Two weeks later we played San Francisco, the defending Super Bowl champions. We dominated them, 26–10. We handed the Dallas Cowboys their worst loss ever, 44–0. We clinched the NFC Central Division title in week eleven, with more than a month left in the regular season.

When our record reached 12–0, the question became "Can the Bears go undefeated?" Only one team in NFL history, the 1972 Dolphins, had gone through an entire season unbeaten and untied. Suddenly, we were on the threshold. That possibility was all the media could talk about, especially in Chicago and Miami.

We probably should have known what was coming when, in week thirteen, we flew to Miami to play the Dolphins. Don Shula coached the 1972 Dolphins and was still coaching the team. He is very protective of that 1972 team's place in NFL history and was determined to knock us off that night in the Orange Bowl.

There was so much hype surrounding the game, it was like a mini–Super Bowl. It drew the largest TV audience in the history of Monday Night Football. We wound up losing, 28–24, as Dan Marino beat our blitzing defense with three touchdown passes. Shula did a masterful coaching job; we did not.

It was a disappointment, but I think it may have helped us achieve the larger goal, which was winning the Super Bowl. The sting of losing seemed to refocus everyone, including the coaches. We realized we weren't invincible after all. Guys rolled up their sleeves and went back to work.

By the time we got to the Super Bowl, which was held in New Orleans, there was almost a circus atmosphere surrounding our team. The Super Bowl Shuffle was the number-one-selling video in the country. Perry was in demand for every commercial and talk show on the air. McMahon was feuding with the league office over the words printed on his headband.

One week the word was "Adidas," the sporting goods company he represented at the time. The league hit him with a five-thousand-dollar fine for using the headband as an advertising space. The next game McMahon wore a headband with "Rozelle" on it, referring to then–NFL commissioner Pete Rozelle.

When the TV camera came in for a close-up, McMahon stuck out his tongue. I guess he was sticking it out at Rozelle or the league office or authority in general. With Jim, you never knew.

I was in the middle of the whole thing, doing my best to make sure the team remembered what the hell we were trying to accomplish: winning the NFL championship.

The night before the Super Bowl, I tried to put things into perspective. Rather than tell the players what the game meant, I asked them to tell me what it meant to them.

I figured they were tired of listening to me. They had heard me almost every day for six months. But I knew they would listen to each other.

I asked, "What does winning the Super Bowl mean to you, Hampton? . . . What is it worth to you, Singletary?"

I went around the room, calling on each guy.

I asked them, "What does this mean to you? What does it mean to your family? How hard are you going to play for the guy next to you? For Walter Payton? For Singletary? For each other?"

I asked Perry what the game was worth to him. So much had come his way that year, with all the commercials and stuff, I wanted to see if he still had his priorities straight. This was a Super Bowl, and he was playing against John Hannah, the best offensive lineman in the league.

I said, "Bill, if you can beat this guy, you can beat anybody." He accepted the challenge. He whipped Hannah's butt. The whole team responded the same way. They played hard and played with a purpose.

I told the team that that game was our defining moment. For that one moment in time, we were the world champions, the very best. This is a big world, and the NFL has been around a long time, so to be able to say you're the best is something really special.

People who never played the game think it's about money, and guys who never won a championship think it's about wearing a Super Bowl ring; but it's not about that. At least, it isn't for me.

To me, it's about someday being able to tell your kids or your grandchildren that at least one time in your life you were the best. How many people can honestly say that? Most people go through their whole lives and do not know how it feels. But when you win a Super Bowl, you have that feeling the rest of your life.

If it's not worth breaking your ass over that, I don't know what is.

I found winning a Super Bowl as a coach more satisfying than winning one as a player because you feel the collective accomplishment. As a player, it is personal. But as a coach, you look at the whole picture and how all the pieces fit together.

The following year I handed out T-shirts with "Are You Satisfied?" printed on them. It was my way of asking the players if they still had the hunger to win another Super Bowl. We didn't get it done, but it was not for a lack of effort.

Injuries killed us in 1986. We lost our two top quarterbacks, McMahon and Mike Tomczak, and still won fifteen of eighteen games before we lost to Washington in an NFC Playoff Game.

We remained a pretty good team for a while. We made the playoffs every season except one from 1986 through 1991. We turned over the roster, usually because of age and injury, but in some cases because a certain player became counterproductive.

Stay True to Your Style

There are people, I know, who did not approve of my coaching style. They thought I ranted and raved too much. They thought I was too tough on my players, that I was too critical at times.

If anybody expects me to apologize, he's going to be disappointed. I was not perfect. I made mistakes, the same as everyone else does. But I did the best I could and did it the only way I knew how — my way.

I was tough, demanding, and all that, but so was Lombardi, so was Knute Rockne, so was Woody Hayes — and those guys are all right in my book. Those guys won, too, so there must be something to it.

I'm a fierce competitor. I've been that way my whole life, even when I was a kid in Aliquippa, Pennsylvania. I didn't have many friends in Little League, because I hated to lose. If another kid on the team made an error, I kicked him out of his position and took over. If our pitcher walked too many guys, I came in and pitched.

I know the other kids didn't like it, but I was not going to stand around and watch us lose. I played to win and, when I became a coach, coached to win.

Players who had the same attitude never had a problem with me. But if a guy lacked discipline or didn't feel like putting out, yeah, I chewed him out. Damn right, I did. I cannot respect people like that.

"Underachiever" is a big word these days. I hear it in football, in business, in schools, all over the place. Obviously, there are a lot of people in all walks of life who have ability and are not making the most of it.

But it could be that the people on top are doing a lousy job of telling the underachievers what is expected of them. A guy might not spend the extra hour studying film unless you, as the head coach or as the boss, tell him it is important. A player might not think weighing an extra ten pounds is a big deal unless you tell him it is costing him a step on every play.

I didn't shout at players to hurt their feelings. I did it hoping to make them better. I criticized Perry a lot and I liked Perry, but he hurt himself by carrying too much weight. I was tough on cornerback Donnell Woolford because I knew that he had great talent but did not seem to understand that pro football is a business and, like any business, is something you have to work at every day.

In the last conversation I had with Donnell, right after I left the Bears, I told him, "You can be a great player. It's up to you." He is showing signs of it now, and I'm happy for him.

I was excitable as a coach. I've seen enough film of myself to know it is true. I also had a heart attack in November of 1988 when I was only forty-nine years old. I learned a lot about myself after the heart attack.

Mostly I learned I cannot change the way I am.

After the heart attack, I promised everyone, especially my wife, Diane, and my cardiologist, Dr. Jay Alexander, that I would slow down, stop working so hard, and quit smoking cigars. I told the press, "I'm going to control my temper. You'll be so amazed, you will think I'm Friar Tuck."

But I wasn't meant to be Friar Tuck any more than I was meant to be Tom Landry. How the hell was I going to change after being one way my whole life?

I was off cigars for three weeks; then I went back to them. I figured it this way: It won't be cigars that kill me. It will be stress, and it might not even be football stress or work stress; it might be missing a three-foot putt for par. Or losing at cards.

Competition is just such a part of me that I don't see myself ever changing. After my heart attack I spoke with Coach Landry and remember saying, "I can't control what happens on the field. Once the game starts, it's up to the players. There is no use getting upset. It ain't that important."

It sounded good, and at the time I really believed it. But once I got back to work and the juices started flowing, I went back to being the same old nutty guy.

I took increasingly more criticism for my sidelines behavior and my occasional outbursts with the media in my last few years as coach. I think the fact that we were not winning as much was the reason. When we were a Super Bowl team, I did the same things and was called "fiery." But when we started to lose, people went the other way and said, "That Ditka is out of control."

It made me angry, all that negative stuff, but now I see it for what it was and take it with a grain of salt. You have to be true to yourself, and I was. I could have handled some situations better, but that was true in the Super Bowl season, too, and no one seemed to mind.

The incident everyone remembers was my chewing out quarterback Jim Harbaugh in a 1992 game at Minnesota. If that play had not happened, I still could be coaching the Bears; I really believe that. That one play turned our whole season around, and my life with it.

We were winning, 20–0, and had the game under control until Harbaugh threw an interception that was returned for a touchdown. That play made the score only 20–7, but as soon as it happened I knew we were going to lose the game. It destroyed our confidence. After that play, the Vikings chewed our defense up and spit it out.

If it was a case of Harbaugh just throwing a bad pass, I could have lived with it. Physical mistakes are part of the game. But this was a dumb pass.

Harbaugh audibled out of a long pass play, changing it to a short pass to Neal Anderson, our halfback. But it was so noisy inside the Metrodome that Anderson never heard the audible and never looked for the ball. The result: Harbaugh's pass went right to a Minnesota defender, who had a clear path to the end zone.

We had stressed in our pregame meeting with Harbaugh that because of the noise factor, we did not want him calling audibles. We could not have been more clear about it. So we get ahead, 20–0, and what does he do?

I could live to be a thousand and never understand why he did it. What is the thought process of an individual who knowingly goes against what has been successful? Harbaugh went away from a play that may have scored a touchdown to call a pass play that, even if it was completed, would have gained five yards.

It made no sense, yet he did it and went against our instructions in the process.

I tore into Harbaugh when he came to the bench. The TV camera was on us and they put the picture on the message board in the Metrodome. The crowd went crazy, and that just added fuel to the Vikings' fire.

After we lost, 21–20, the film clip of me chewing out Harbaugh was replayed on every highlight show in the country. It became a major news story and, because we continued to lose, never went away. It probably turned some people against me and made it easier for the club to fire me at the end of the 5–11 season.

Looking back, I could have handled the situation better. I definitely overreacted. That was what Harbaugh said: "You didn't have to act that way." Yeah, but I was right. I may have been too emotional in saying it, but I was right.

That year was difficult, especially the second half when things started to go downhill. For the first time in my life, I did not enjoy going to work. I saw the handwriting on the wall around midseason when I realized I no longer had the backing of the top people in the organization. I wound up on an island — not a good place to be within any business group.

I lost my enthusiasm, and the one thing I always preach is that you must be enthusiastic about your work. I lost all my enthusiasm the last six weeks of the season. I could blame it on the situation and management, but that's a cop-out. I lost it. It was me who lost it. It was time for a change, for both me and the Bears.

Since I've been out of coaching, I've met hundreds of people at my restaurant or through my television work who want me to get back in. I believe most people like what I stand for. They know I don't tolerate monkey business and phoniness.

For the ones who don't like me, tough. I'm not going to change.

Turning a Team Around

Dennis Green

HEAD COACH

MINNESOTA VIKINGS, 1992—PRESENT

When Dennis Green was hired in 1992, the Minnesota Vikings were an aging and troubled team, riddled by dissension. In his first year Green made a dramatic sweep of the roster, cutting a number of big-name veterans and bringing in seventeen new faces.

He instilled a sense of discipline and order in the team and, in the process, led the Vikings to an 11–5 regular season record and a first-place finish in the NFC Central Division. He was named NFL Coach of the Year by United Press International and the Washington Touchdown Club.

"The team needed to be reenergized, to be motivated, to have individualism taken out of the equation," says Vikings president Roger Headrick. "Dennis was the right man for the job. He just knows how to get people to work for him."

Green, now forty-six, has shown leadership skills from an early age. He served as class president in high school and worked as a crew chief on a maintenance job when he was seventeen, giving orders to men twice his age.

The youngest of five brothers, Green grew up in Harrisburg, Pennsylvania, where he was an all-state halfback at John Harris High School. He went to the University of Iowa, where he earned a degree in recreation education and made honorable mention All–Big Ten as a running back.

After college Green played one season with the British Columbia Lions of the Canadian Football League. He returned to Iowa as a graduate assistant; because he was married with two children, he had to take a second job driving a truck for a sheet-metal company from dawn until noon.

Green became a full-time assistant coach at the University of Dayton in 1973. He went back to Iowa for the next two seasons and then got his big break in 1977 when Bill Walsh hired him as backfield coach at Stanford. In 1979 Walsh became head coach in San Francisco and brought Green with him.

"Dennis has always had a great sense of maturity, a great sense of purpose, and a great sense of dedication," Walsh says. "But as much as anything else, he thinks clearly under pressure. He is almost a case study in successful coaching."

Green's first head-coach opportunity came in 1981 when he was hired at Northwestern, a school that was in the midst of the longest losing streak in Division I football. He took the job even though friends urged him not to, characterizing the situation at Northwestern as hopeless.

After an 0–11 first season, Green was honored as Big Ten Coach of the Year in 1982 by leading the Wildcats to three victories, including an upset of Michigan State in East Lansing.

Green returned to the 49ers in 1986 as receivers coach and was on the staff when San Francisco won Super Bowl XXIII.

In 1989 Green took on the task of rebuilding Stanford's football program, which had fallen on hard times. In his third year, 1991, Green led the Cardinal to an 8–3 record, which included a seven-game winning streak, the school's longest in forty years.

"Dennis revolutionized Stanford football," says Andy Geiger, Stanford's former athletic director. "He is a superb corporate executive. That's what we all look for. A lot of people can X and O you to death, but inside, their program is a shambles.

"With Dennis, you get soup to nuts, A to Z. Football is

America's corporate game. It's all about organization and motivation, and those are areas in which Dennis excels."

The Vikings recognized that ability and hired Green in January 1992, making him only the second black head coach in pro football's modern era.

When I was hired as head coach of the Minnesota Vikings, I made a statement at my first press conference that probably seemed a little brash.

Facing a room full of reporters and TV cameras, I announced, "There's a new sheriff in town."

I said it with a smile, but I also said it with a purpose.

I wanted to make it clear, right from the start, that things were going to change with the Vikings. The sooner everyone understood that, the better.

When I arrived, the Vikings were a team loaded with big-name, high-salaried players, but they were not winning. They had missed the playoffs the two previous seasons, and there was a lot of bickering and cliquishness within the team and, really, the whole organization.

I was coming in from the outside, having spent the previous three years as head coach at Stanford. I had talked to some friends in the league about the Vikings, and they all said the same thing: it was a team with talent, but it lacked discipline. It didn't play hard every week.

There were quite a few veteran players on the roster who were getting by on reputation. They had good credentials — many of them had appeared in the Pro Bowl — but they had settled into a comfort zone where they worked just hard enough to get by. They were jaded, and their play reflected it. My job was to turn the team around; and to do that, I first had to adjust the attitude. Talking about change was not enough. I had to make moves and shake things up.

I knew there would be some resistance and perhaps some

criticism in the media, but I wasn't worried about it. Being the head of a football team or a business is not a popularity contest. Worrying about whether people like you or agree with you is a mistake.

Whether you are hired to turn around a faltering football team or a faltering corporation, you cannot lose sight of the obvious. You were brought in because the system is not working and, as the new honcho, you have to fix what's broken. That may mean changing personnel or may mean changing the physical plant and turning the whole operation inside out. You may find it necessary to change work schedules or to juggle shifts to improve production, to get things moving. Some people will resist, but that's human nature. Most of us are leery of change.

As the new man in charge, you have to be right on top of things. You have to convince the workers, or players, that you know what you're doing and that while things are going to change around the workplace, those who stay will see that it is for the better.

The issue is not trying to get unanimous approval or to get elected man of the year. It is doing what you think is right. I was involved in rebuilding programs at two Division I colleges, Northwestern and Stanford, so I knew what taking over in Minnesota entailed.

You must have two things: a clear plan on how to rebuild and the courage to stick with it. In other words, you can talk the sheriff talk, but you'd better be able to walk the sheriff walk. And you may have to dodge a few bullets along the way.

My objective as head coach was to establish a criterion, a mode of operation that was part of the daily routine, and to set a certain tempo for the whole organization. Once that's done, you have a foundation you can build on.

The Vikings had been practicing the same way for about twenty years under head coaches Bud Grant and Jerry Burns. While it may have worked at one time, it wasn't working anymore. The team was 24–24 in the three seasons prior to my arrival. The system had grown stale, and some players had grown stale with it. I had to break the team out of that lethargy before we could begin moving forward.

I started the first day of our spring minicamp. I noticed that when the players finished their stretching exercises and broke down for group drills, most of them walked or jogged leisurely to their respective fields. They did it routinely. The Vikings had done it that way for years.

I blew my whistle and called them back. I said that from now on, all players would run from drill to drill. I made them start practice over again, beginning with the calisthenics.

The next day, one unnamed player was quoted in the newspaper calling me a "college coach" with a lot of stupid rah-rah ideas.

It didn't surprise me. I knew some of the veterans would resent my methods. I didn't care because they were the players I wanted to weed out anyway.

It may seem like a small thing — making the players run from drill to drill, making them repeat their calisthenics — but it sent a clear message to the team that what was good enough before wasn't good enough now. I let the players know immediately where I was coming from. That positioning is very important.

In football, as in business, a tone is set by the man on top, whether he is the head coach, the president, or the chairman of the board. My emphasis was twofold. One, this is a business and we ought to be good at it. Two, we should be willing to work at it and still enjoy what we do. Ideally, the two should go hand-in-hand.

When you are trying to turn around a losing situation, you have to start with a thorough and honest assessment of what it is you are inheriting. Obviously, not everything is going to be good; but not everything is going to be bad, either. I spent a lot of time studying the roster and looking for the "keepers."

The Vikings were labeled underachievers by many people, but there were some terrific players on the team, such as guard Randall McDaniel, wide receiver Cris Carter, and running back Terry Allen [released in the 1995 offseason]. They were a big part of the nucleus that I kept in 1992 and have been major contributors to our rise as a playoff team.

As a new head coach coming in with a mandate for change, there is nothing more important than choosing the right personnel. If you pick the best players, the team sees what you are doing and develops confidence. But if you keep players for other reasons, such as reputation, salary, or politics, then people inside and outside the team begin to wonder if you really have the guts to get the job done. Once that doubt sets in, you're in trouble.

My first year in Minnesota, I made the decision to either trade or release four high-profile veterans: running back Herschel Walker, safety Joey Browner, defensive tackle Keith Millard, and quarterback Wade Wilson. All four were excellent players at one time (they appeared in a combined ten Pro Bowls), but I felt the team was better off moving in another direction.

I saw the Vikings as a collection of players that at one time probably did have a chance to go to the Super Bowl and maybe win it, but that time had come and gone by 1991. They had their shots in 1987 and 1988 and couldn't get over the hump. All they had done since then was get older. I knew it was time to bring in new blood.

I was asked time and again, "How can you let Herschel Walker go? He led the team in rushing the last three years. How can you let Wade Wilson go? He took the team to the NFC Championship Game."

I pointed out that it was 1992 and that Wilson took the Vikings to the NFC title game in January 1988. Four seasons had passed, and the team had gone steadily backward. Wilson was thirty-three, and we had two young quarterbacks, Rich Gannon and Sean Salisbury, who needed a chance to prove themselves.

Walker was a unique case because the team had given up so much to acquire him in a trade with Dallas in 1989. And if you went strictly by the statistics, Walker had been a productive player, leading the Vikings in yards rushing three consecutive years.

But I looked at the bottom line.

What did Walker's yards mean in the grand scheme of things? In his three seasons in Minnesota, the Vikings were a .500 team and advanced to the playoffs only once, losing to San Francisco, 41–13, in a first-round playoff game in 1990.

I wasn't blaming Herschel, nor was I suggesting that he couldn't play in the NFL. He certainly played well after he left Minnesota. But Walker was twenty-nine at the time, and we had Allen coming along, who was faster and a better fit for what I wanted to do offensively.

Look at the numbers: In 1992 Allen rushed for 1,201 yards and scored fifteen touchdowns. In 1994 he rushed for 1,031 yards and eight touchdowns. We were a playoff team each season. Could Walker have given us all that? It is very unlikely, and that's the whole point.

That is what I mean about having a plan that goes beyond winning one or two more games. One thing I learned working as an assistant coach under Bill Walsh with the 49ers is you don't build championship teams with the blueprint for a 9–7 team.

You make a mistake when you hang on to a player, such as Wilson or Walker, because he is a veteran and knows the system. The bottom line is production: What had the Vikings offense produced with those two players in featured roles? What had the defense produced with Millard and Browner?

It is better, coming in as a new head coach, to cut some of those old ties and give an opportunity to a young player such as Allen, who might become the kind of running back who can lift a team to the Super Bowl, similar to what Roger Craig did when he was with San Francisco.

The Team Concept

I was very up-front when I took over the Vikings. I said we want to be a team on the rise, and you only can achieve that with a team concept. In the past the Vikings had a lot of stars — they sent nine players to the 1988 Pro Bowl — but they did not work together as a team.

My objective was fewer stars, better chemistry, and more victories. We accomplished that. My first season in Minnesota, we had seventeen new faces on the roster and won the NFC Central Division title with an 11–5 record.

When I came to Minnesota, I made an effort to get out in the community and talk with people. I spoke to every Rotary Club in the Twin Cities. I wanted to hear what they thought of the Vikings and also wanted to let them hear my plans, first-hand. What I heard from the fans was mostly frustration. That did not surprise me because some five thousand people had canceled their season tickets after the 1991 season.

One man said something that really stuck with me. He said he had been a season-ticket holder since the Vikings were founded in 1961 and had supported the team through the four Super Bowl losses, but he was ready to give up after the 1991 season.

He said, "I could accept losing, but it broke my heart when they didn't even try."

I promised him that attitude would change. I said as long as I was coach of the Vikings, the team would play hard every week. We might not win every week, but there never would be a question about our effort. I meant that and have done my best to instill that commitment in our team.

Winning stems from commitment, and commitment begins with attitude. That has been true since the beginning of time. If you take over an operation where the attitude stinks, you have to address that situation first before you can begin solving the other problems.

I was very aggressive in that regard when I was hired in Minnesota. The team had a negative image, and rightly so. There were so many cliques on the team, it wasn't like a team at all. There was tremendous jealousy over salaries, which isn't unusual in pro sports. But with the Vikings it took on racial overtones when Browner said he felt there were two pay scales: one for the white stars, and a lower one for the black stars.

Browner later said his remarks were taken out of context, which may be true, but the damage was done already. The chemistry of the team was never the same after that.

Also several players were arrested for incidents around town — drunk driving, fighting, disorderly conduct. So many distractions, so little focus. Was it any surprise the Vikings often performed badly, despite their array of stars?

There has to be a closeness within a team for it to succeed. To me, it was no coincidence that the Vikings had lost ten of sixteen road games in 1990–91 and that the team had a very poor record of coming from behind in the fourth quarter.

Those are situations, when you are backed into a corner in a hostile setting, where the only strength a team has is what it draws from one player supporting another. If that bond isn't there, you will not win many of those close games. Instead, you will wind up with a lot of individuals tossing the blame around, which is what was happening on the Vikings.

I wanted to get back to what the Vikings were in the 1960s and 1970s under Bud Grant. That team took the field with an air of dominance, that they were going to play better than the other guy. They had the ability to turn it up a notch, if necessary. They were admired for that.

Back then, the team had a slogan: "Forty for sixty." That meant forty players giving maximum effort for sixty minutes. As a coach, if you can get that, you will win a lot of games in any era.

When I was hired by the Vikings, I had to sort out this internal mess before I started dealing with Xs and Os. I did some things that, at the time, people thought were nitpicky but that I felt had merit because they set a tone.

Making the players run between drills was one.

Another was rearranging the lockers at our training facility. Before, they were grouped by position: offensive linemen here, defensive backs over there, and so on. I changed the lockers to numerical order, so that while we still had most of the backs in the twenties and the receivers in the eighties, there would be a cornerback between two running backs, and an offensive guard between two defensive linemen.

Some of these guys had been teammates for years and hardly had spoken to each other, because one hung out with his guys and the other hung out with his guys. It was healthy to break those cliques down and see some new friendships develop.

I gave a speech one day where I made the point that "There were too many things going on here in the past that forced people to choose sides. The way I see it, there is only one side. We're all in this together."

Looking around the room, I could see in their faces — most of them, anyway — that I was getting through.

I made it mandatory that every player would have a roommate on road trips. In the past players could pay for a private room if they desired. Private rooms? What is this, golf? Football is the ultimate team sport. I saw no point in indulging an individualistic mentality.

I also asked management if it would pay to have breakfast served at the training facility each morning. This accomplished two things. First, it guaranteed a player would have a decent breakfast to start the day, not a stale doughnut that he grabbed on his way out the door at home. Second, it brought guys to the complex earlier, where they sat around, eating and shooting the breeze for a while before we got down to business.

It was not very long before I could see a difference. The players became closer. The atmosphere became happier, more productive. The team began to look, act, and feel like a team.

Once I had accomplished that initial objective, once I had everyone on the same side, I could say, "Okay, now it's time to go to the blackboard and put in some plays." Now they had a good chance to work. Before, I couldn't be sure.

The highlight of my first season was a 21–20 come-from-behind victory over Chicago. We were trailing, 20–0, but we rallied to score three touchdowns in the final fourteen minutes to win the game. That really sparked our drive to the playoffs.

After the game Tim Irwin, our offensive tackle, made a statement that really told me we were on the right track. Talking about the twenty-point deficit, Tim said, "In the past, we would have turned on each other. Today, we turned on the Bears."

I knew then that we were on our way.

The team concept relates across the board, to business, to government, to any sort of endeavor, because at some level it is all cooperative. We're all part of a team in some way. We all have people to answer to and work with. The smoother those gears mesh, the better for everyone.

I tell my players that everything we do has to reflect a closeness. If it's good for me, it has to be good for you, and vice versa. As head of the operation, I can't be worrying more about the defense than the offense, or bending over backward to accommodate one player and not the others. That's lousy coaching and, in a business sense, lousy management.

My general rule, which I have followed throughout my coaching career, is that everyone doesn't necessarily get treated the same way, because I'm not sure that's possible. But everyone has to be treated fairly. Moreover, they have to know and trust that they will be treated fairly.

I sometimes compare the team to a ship preparing to leave port. I tell the players, "You can get aboard, but don't slow us down." In other words, there are no passengers. Everybody grabs an oar and pulls — it doesn't matter if he's making a million dollars or the league minimum.

Once you set that as a standard, as head coach it is up to you to enforce it. A common mistake made by some coaches is they let their superstars write their own rules. Don't feel like lifting weights today? Fine, skip it. You want to leave practice early to tape a TV show? Sure, no big deal.

If you built your program on teamwork and togetherness, as I did, you have to make the principle of "team" stick. If you don't, the players will tune you out, the rifts probably will reappear in the locker room, and you will be in an even deeper mess than when you started.

Let me relate a story.

In 1981 I accepted the job as head football coach at Northwestern. At the time Northwestern was the most downtrodden Division I program in the nation. The team had not won a game in two seasons and, because of its strict academic standards, was at a huge disadvantage recruiting players against the rest of the Big Ten schools.

One of the few blue-chip players I inherited was Chris Hinton, a tight end who had just completed his sophomore season. He probably was the best football player to come through Northwestern in two decades, and he has been starting for me at offensive tackle with the Vikings. But I'm getting ahead of myself.

At spring practice I looked at the squad, and in terms of physical ability, Hinton was head and shoulders above the rest. But he was lackadaisical. He did not see the need to push himself. He had slipped into a mind-set that no matter what he did, it wasn't going to make a difference. After all, this was Northwestern — and Northwestern always lost.

Everyone liked Chris. He was a delightful guy — his nickname was "Yogi Bear"— but his work habits stunk. As a coach, I was in an awkward position.

Clearly, he was my best player — even operating at 50 percent. But I was attempting to turn around a losing program and, as I did later with the Vikings, stressed the need for a total commitment from everyone. How could I expect the rest of the team to give it if I let Chris get away with less?

We had a mandatory mile run for the players, and Chris walked part of the way. I called him into my office that afternoon and told him he was off the team.

I gave him John Robinson's phone number at USC. I told him he should do himself a favor and transfer there so he could see what a top-notch college football program was like. I even offered to make the call for him.

I said, "Maybe then you'll live up to your potential. As it is, you are wasting it."

Chris was shaken because he never expected to be kicked off

the losingest team in college football. His pride was deeply hurt. He told me he didn't want to transfer; he wanted to stay at Northwestern. I said fine, but he would not be playing football.

Two weeks passed and Chris called my office three times, pleading for another chance. Finally I agreed to let him come back, but he had to earn his way. I put him on the scout team, which meant he worked against the first unit in practice. He was a different guy, hungrier, with something to prove.

It was a good thing for Chris, and it was a good for the whole team because at that point they understood when I talked about paying the price to win, it meant *everyone* paying the price.

The epilogue to the story is that I switched Chris from tight end to offensive tackle, and he made All-America as a senior. He was the fourth player selected in the 1983 NFL draft and has played twelve outstanding seasons in the league, earning Pro Bowl honors seven times.

If you are the boss, you must have the courage to make those demands. If you shrug your shoulders, look the other way, and say, "Oh well, that's good enough," you never will fix what's wrong with the business.

It does not mean being a tyrant, just someone who understands his responsibility to each individual and the group as a whole.

In football or in business I believe in hiring people who are dependable. I know what you're thinking, "Gee, Dennis, no kidding?"

But you would be surprised how many coaches and executives don't do that. They will take a guy with a bigger name or more God-given ability and not weigh the dependability factor.

I see it in the NFL all the time: players who were number-one draft picks, guys with all the physical tools, bouncing from team to team. Why?

Because once you get past the physical ability, the guy is a slacker. He has lousy work habits, he doesn't concentrate, he doesn't compete. That type of individual is very detrimental to a team. Not only does he fail to do his job, but he hurts the team, because the other players cannot count on him from one play to the next.

I would rather have a player of average ability who always gives 100 percent than a player of superior ability who gives 100 percent only when he's in the mood. I know the first guy can be counted on, and his teammates know it, too.

Our roster reflects that. Some of our best players were considered marginal athletes at one time. Terry Allen was a ninth-round draft pick. John Randle, our all-pro defensive tackle, was a free agent out of a small college, Texas A & I. James Harris, who starts at defensive end, was a free agent after being cut by Seattle. They all were considered too small, too slow, too something. But I wanted them on our team because they gave every ounce of their ability every time they walked on the field.

We played a game in 1994 against Miami, and the Dolphins had eight first-round draft picks on offense — eight out of eleven players. We lined up with a defense that had no first-round picks and four free agents. You would say that on paper it was a mismatch, yet we won the game. We won because we played hard, we played physical, and we played as a team.

Plan Your Work, Work Your Plan

I have an expression: "Plan your work, work your plan." By that I mean, know what you want to do and then don't deviate. Because if there's one thing I've learned, both in football and in life, it's that there's no textbook for leadership. Sometimes you have to go on your instincts and find a way to get things done that other people may consider unorthodox. Well, if it works, who cares?

I had to work from an early age. Both of my parents were deceased by the time I was thirteen, so I was raised by my four older brothers. We all worked to bring in money, and in high school I got a job at the Harrisburg, Pennsylvania, airport.

Because I was going to school and playing sports, I worked the overnight shift, 11:00 P.M. to 7:00 A.M., when the airport was closed. Although I was only seventeen, I was put in charge of a crew of six men, all older than me.

When I was hired, I was told the crew was doing a bad job, that the guys obviously were goofing off because they had the airport to themselves and still things were not getting done. I was supposed to whip them into shape.

I did not want to come in cracking a whip, but I had to find a way to improve job performance. So I came up with a plan. I bought an alarm clock and brought it to work. I set it for 2:00 A.M. I told the guys, "We'll really bear down and work for three hours. Then from two o'clock until five, you can do whatever you want. Sleep, eat, watch TV, I don't care. I'll set the alarm again for five. Then we go back to work for the last two hours." The last two hours, from 5:00 to 7:00 A.M., were when we did the windows because that was when the sun came up. It made sense to me, and it worked.

Some people will say that this plan was ridiculous, building in a three-hour time block for what amounted to goofing off. I would argue they are missing the point. Forget the three hours off. Look at what was accomplished in the other five hours.

We got an excellent efficiency rating, and the guys were perfectly happy because they knew they could count on that two-to-five break. They were good workers. All they needed was someone to structure their time.

Part of good management is knowing how to size up a job and the available resources and then to figure out the best way to make it work. What may work in one situation may fall flat in another. You have to be flexible enough to recognize the difference.

My head-coach jobs at Northwestern and Stanford, while similar to the Vikings in the sense that the programs were down and needed to be turned around, were a different challenge for me. Tougher in some ways — and in the case of Northwestern, much riskier.

As I mentioned earlier, Northwestern had not won a game in two years when I was offered the head-coach job in 1981. At the time I was offensive coordinator at Stanford. Previously, I had been an assistant coach with the 49ers under Walsh. I was thirty-one with a pretty good résumé.

When I received the Northwestern offer, all I heard from other coaches was "Don't do it. The place is a graveyard." The consensus was that if I went there, I would either sink my coaching career or at the very least set it back ten years.

There was another issue involved: race. As an African-American, I was well aware there were very few black head coaches in Division I football and the NFL. The number is pitifully small, even today.

Some people, who meant well I'm sure, argued against my taking over a program as troubled as the one at Northwestern, fearing that if I went there and was just another losing coach and got fired, it might hurt the chances of other black coaches to advance.

Whether that was true or not, I don't know; but it was not something I dismissed casually. I knew there was a lot riding on my decision, yet I felt there was no way I could turn down the job. I saw it as an opportunity. Sometimes you have to be willing to take a job no one else will take. I don't think you can sit back and wait for what you think is the easiest path to success.

I could have waited until Michigan or USC or one of those powerhouse schools knocked on my door, just like you could wait until a Fortune 500 company calls and offers you an executive position. But how likely is that?

I saw this as a first step up the ladder, albeit a difficult one. I had confidence in my ability to put a competitive team on the field at Northwestern, even if we never made it to the powerhouse level.

It was hard, even harder than I had imagined. In my first year we did not win a game. We went 0–11. It was a different experience for me because I learned to take my ego totally out of the equation. We were not going to win a national title, but we stressed playing hard and playing with pride, no matter what the outcome.

At one point in my second season, our losing streak reached thirty-four games, which was the longest in the nation, but the team continued to play hard. When we finally did win a few games (we were 3–8 that second season), I was voted Big Ten Coach of the Year.

When I took over the Stanford program in 1989, it was down, but not as far down as Northwestern's had been. Stanford had a winning tradition. The academic standards were high at Stanford, but it was easier to recruit good athletes because, unlike Northwestern, Stanford was a school the NFL teams regularly scouted and tapped for talent.

In my three seasons as head coach, the Cardinal went from 3–8 to 5–6 to 8–4. The highlight of my final year was a 36–31 upset of Notre Dame on the road when the Irish were ranked number one in the nation.

What really made me proud was when pro scouts and personnel directors, such as Bobby Beathard, now with San Diego, came in to scout our team. Beathard once told me, "I'll take one of your players anytime. They know how to practice and play."

That comment told me we were doing our job as coaches. To me, it spoke even louder than the improvement in our record.

The parallel I would draw to business is that you can make huge strides in a relatively short time if you create the proper atmosphere. Many of the players who helped us beat Notre Dame in 1991 were the same players who could not make a first down against Oregon State three years earlier.

As a new head coach or top executive, you will make some sweeping changes to start, and that is important. But after the first wave of change, there must evolve a clearly defined sense of "This is what we want to do and this is how we will do it." Once you have a framework, you can develop the people, or players, in the program and really maximize their abilities.

I have not mentioned much about race to this point and really don't want to focus on it. Almost every interview I've done as a head coach, either in college or with the Vikings, has dealt with it to some degree, however. I wish it no longer was an issue. It shouldn't be, but it still is.

There were only two black head coaches in Division I football in the 1994 season, and there are now only two in the NFL, me and Ray Rhodes, who took over the Eagles in 1995. Art Shell was head coach of the Los Angeles Raiders from 1989 to 1994. There should be more, and I really believe in the near future there will be more.

The Vikings did not hire me because I was black. They hired me because they felt, from what I'd done at the college level, I had the know-how to lift the franchise out of its rut. I did not ask for any special treatment, nor did I ask to be judged any differently than any other head coach. Judge me by my record, the wins and the losses. That is how it should be.

I've heard it said that because I'm an African-American, I can get more out of black players. That is nonsense. The color of one's skin doesn't matter. Preparation and competence is what matters. Players won't play any harder because of race. They don't want a black man or a white man to lead them. They want a man who knows what he is doing. I do my damnedest to be that man.

The Three Ds

There are some basic principles I incorporate in coaching, things I feel are applicable to an executive position in any business. These are the three Ds: desire, dedication, and determination.

Desire is the essence of learning. It establishes exactly what you want.

Dedication is the price you have to pay to get what you want. You may want to play pro football, but so do a thousand other guys. There is a price you have to pay to make it, including time in the weight room, time spent working on technique, time in film study. That is the dedication factor.

If desire is what we want and dedication is the price we have to pay to get what we want, then determination is what keeps us there. I tell players, "It's no disgrace to get knocked down. It's only a disgrace if you don't get back up." Determination is what keeps you getting up.

We all can relate to these three values because we all need them to be successful. And success begins with setting goals. I've always defined goals as SMART: specific, measurable, attainable, realistic, and timely.

Specific means clear-cut. Make sure everyone knows what is expected of him. It does no good to tell your staff, "Hey, gang, we've got to show a better return this quarter." It would be the same as me telling our squad, "This week, we need to make more big plays."

The players would be thinking, "Okay, tell us how. What are we going to do?" In other words, be specific.

As the man in charge, you must have it right at your fingertips: "We will attack it in the following ways. We are going to pass more on first down. We're going to try to isolate this receiver on this defender. That means we'll need better pass protection from you linemen because the pattern takes time to develop . . ." and so on. Once your workforce knows exactly what is expected of it, then everything comes down to execution.

Are our goals measurable? In football they are, absolutely. At the end of a season, we're either in the playoffs or we're not. If we're 6–10, something is wrong.

On the Vikings we set measurable objectives. Our primary goal each season is to make the playoffs. Our other objectives include being in the top five in our conference in offense, the top seven in defense, and the top six in special teams. We set other goals, such as increasing our home attendance and our national TV appearances.

All those goals are measurable. Week to week, you know exactly where you stand, where you need to improve, and whether your efficiency level is going up or down. You might not like what you see all the time, but at least you know where you are in relation to the competition.

Are the goals attainable? I see to it that they are. Otherwise, what's the point?

That's not to say the goals should be easy. They should reflect what your team is capable of doing when it is functioning properly, not at 60 percent or 70 percent of its ability.

For example, we lost our opening game in 1994, 16–10, to Green Bay. It was a disappointing performance, especially because it was our first game with Warren Moon at quarterback. When I went over the film with our squad, I focused on one thing: dropped passes.

Our receivers dropped eight balls that Warren put right in their hands. I pointed out that each of those potential catches would have given us a first down. That's at least three more offensive plays. Multiply three plays times eight drops and that's twenty-four offensive plays we should have had. That's twenty-four chances to score points that we simply gave away.

So the goal I set for the team was to score more points. Was it attainable? Sure, all they had to do was hold on to the football when it hit them in the hands. Two weeks later, we scored forty-two points against Chicago. The week after that, we scored thirty-eight against Miami.

Are the goals realistic? My first season in Minnesota, I set the playoffs as a goal because I felt it was realistic. We won the division title with eleven regular-season victories. My second season we made it again, this time as a wild-card team.

I felt those were realistic goals, and we reached them. In 1994 I set the playoffs as our first goal, but I also talked to the squad about going to the Super Bowl. We felt we had the talent and the experience to make a big-time run at it.

I was not afraid to talk about the Super Bowl with our players. If you are afraid to say it, you surely cannot do it. I feel we are very close to that level. It is important that the players feel it as well.

Once, at Northwestern we played one of the Big Ten powerhouse teams and played them pretty well for about a quarter. We had two or three shots to score points, came away with nothing, and wound up losing by something like 40–10.

In my postgame press conference, I remarked, "It's hard to believe at one time the score was 0–0." People thought I was being sarcastic or funny, but I really wasn't. What I meant was that our players started in a hole psychologically because they really didn't think they had a chance to win. They weren't ready to seize the opportunity when it presented itself.

That's where the timing comes in. You have to set goals that reflect the situation. If there is a sense of urgency, as there often is in football, your goals as a team had better reflect it.

Let me illustrate with a scenario we faced late in the 1993 season. We had a very tough year with a lot of injuries and were 6–7 with three weeks left in the regular season. We had to win all three games to have any chances of reaching our overall goal, which was making the playoffs.

It was going to be a difficult task with two of the three games on the road and two of them against teams with better records. We were to play, in order, Green Bay, Kansas City, and Washington. I don't think anyone outside the team itself thought we had a prayer of winning all three games.

In talking to the squad, I compared this challenge to a door, the door to the land of opportunity. I said we had to force it open a crack by beating Green Bay; then we had to open it a little wider by beating Kansas City; then we could kick it open by winning the last game against Washington, which was the weakest team of the three.

On the other side of the door was the playoffs.

That week we played a very gutty game and beat the Packers, 21–17. I told the team afterward, "There is the crack in the door."

The next week we played the Chiefs with Joe Montana. If we won it, we were 8–7. Still no guarantee of making the playoffs, but we'd be alive and would be gaining confidence. We responded by playing our best game of the year, winning 30–10.

Going into the final week, I did not have to say very much. By then the door was two-thirds of the way open. Even though our last game was to be played in Washington, where the Vikings had not won since 1980, I felt confident. We won, 14–9, to finish 9–7 and earn a wild-card spot in the playoffs.

The land of opportunity is something I learned about from my grandmother. She was a small, Southern woman with a limited formal education. But she was deeply religious and very wise.

She would say that you have to be prepared at all times because you never know when opportunity will come your way. She talked about the door and how you never know when it will open. You can't wait for it to open, then say, "Let me get my bags packed. I'll be right back."

By the time you do, the door will be shut and the opportunity lost. This metaphor applies to every aspect of business and sports. It is like a backup quarterback who dreams of being a starter. He must practice hard and study his playbook because he never knows when the number-one guy will go down and, suddenly, it is his game.

He can't say, "Give me a few minutes, coach. I need to look over the game plan." When the door to opportunity opens, the clock starts ticking. That backup quarterback has to be ready. We all do.

Starting from Square One

Tom Coughlin

HEAD COACH

JACKSONVILLE JAGUARS, 1995—PRESENT

Boston Globe columnist Dan Shaughnessy once described Tom Coughlin as "RoboCoach, equal parts Lombardi, Patton, and Nixon." Coughlin's intensity helped convince Jacksonville owner Wayne Weaver to make him the first head coach of the expansion Jaguars, which began play in the NFL in 1995.

"We interviewed a lot of people, but we did not offer the job to anyone else," Weaver says. "People had great things to say about Tom. Bill Parcells said, 'He is one of the three best coaches I've ever worked with,' which was quite a testimonial."

Coughlin was a receivers coach under Parcells with the New York Giants from 1988 through 1990. He was with the Giants when they won Super Bowl XXV, 20–19, against Buffalo. He took over at Boston College the following year.

There, Coughlin inherited a faltering football program and, within two years, restored it to prominence. He did it with a hard-driving diligence that earned him another nickname, "Technical Tom."

Coughlin, forty-eight, grew up in a small town, Waterloo, New York. He went to Syracuse on a football scholarship and played in the same backfield as Larry Csonka and Floyd Little.

Coughlin led the team in receptions one season and won the outstanding scholar-athlete award as a senior.

After earning a master's degree, Coughlin began his coaching career at Rochester (New York) Institute of Technology. He returned to Syracuse as an assistant coach in 1975 and was promoted to offensive coordinator two years later.

In 1980 Coughlin was hired by Boston College as quarterbacks coach. He helped develop Doug Flutie, who won the Heisman Trophy in 1984. Coughlin then went to the NFL as an assistant coach with Philadelphia (1984–85) and Green Bay (1986–87), before joining Parcells's staff in New York.

Coughlin is a tireless worker who is in his office almost every day at 6:00 A.M. and only takes a break for a midafternoon run. He has a strict rule that no one sits down during practice. His teenage daughter Katie came to watch practice one afternoon and when she sat on the bench, her father told her to get up.

"Nobody sits down," he said.

And to Coughlin, "nobody" means nobody.

During his first season at Boston College, Coughlin came down with pneumonia, but never missed a day of practice. It was a reflection of the way he grew up. He worked construction in the summer and ran home from work every day in his steel-toed boots to build up his endurance.

Coughlin's birthday is August 31, but he says he has not celebrated it since he was fourteen. It falls on the eve of the football season, so he cannot afford to take time off. He observes his birthday sometime during the offseason when it does not interfere with his work.

"You don't have to spend a lot of time with Tom to learn that what you see is what you get," Weaver said in an interview. "He is bright and straightforward. We wanted an offensive mind as head coach, and I would say Tom was my first choice."

I've been involved in football for a very long time but never experienced anything like the 1994 season. I was a head coach without a team. I had an office and a title. I even had five assistant coaches. But I did not have any players.

I was head coach of the Jacksonville Jaguars, one of two expansion franchises [the Carolina Panthers is the other] that began play in the National Football League in the 1995 season. I was hired in January 1994 and spent a full year putting the pieces in place so that our team would be ready to meet the challenge.

It was a great experience, but it also was very frustrating.

I worked sixty hours a week but did not have a game to play on Sunday. There is nothing like the excitement of game day. I missed it greatly in 1994.

It was a unique opportunity, to have a hand in building an NFL franchise from the ground up. When I was hired by the Jaguars, our offices were in a trailer parked next to our home field, the Gator Bowl. There were six people in the office, including secretaries, and we had eighteen months to assemble a team and put it on the field for our first preseason game.

There were times when I wondered, "What have I gotten into?" There was so much work to be done. We had to find a suitable practice facility and a training-camp site, hire trainers and equipment managers, build a scouting staff, and search for players.

I spent every weekend of the 1994 season on the road, scouting college games on Saturday and pro games on Sunday. My staff of assistant coaches and three scouts also made the rounds, gathering information on potential players.

We wanted to be as prepared as possible for our first NFL draft in 1995 as well as for the expansion draft in which we could select players from a list of veterans made available by the other twenty-eight NFL teams.

Most teams have four or five holes to fill each season. As an expansion team, we had fifty-three holes to fill, one for every spot on the roster.

There were so many decisions to make and so little time. I never worked harder than I did in 1994, but I didn't have a scoreboard to check each Sunday to see if we were on the right track. I had to trust my instincts. I'll find out in our first few seasons just how well we did.

Right now, I'm optimistic. I feel we have done a good job of putting the team together, of assembling an experienced coaching staff, and of scouting the available talent on both the pro and college level. I feel we have a competitive product on the field, but until we play enough games, we won't know for sure.

Keep the Faith

I'm aware of the history of NFL expansion teams. No previous expansion team has won more than three games in its first season. That is a sobering thought, especially for a guy who hates losing more than anything in the world.

The Dallas Cowboys did not win a game their first season, finishing 0–11–1 in 1960. It was not until their seventh season that the Cowboys finished with a winning record. The Tampa Bay Buccaneers joined the league in 1976 and lost their first twenty-six regular-season games. Eleven of the losses were shutouts.

I've talked to the two men who coached those teams, Tom Landry in Dallas and John McKay in Tampa Bay. They said the key to surviving is keeping your faith in yourself. No matter how bleak things may appear, you have to maintain belief in what you're doing as head coach. Lose that and you lose everything. I imagine that the same advice would hold true when starting a business.

As a new team, we are at a tremendous disadvantage playing against teams the caliber of the Pittsburgh Steelers, Green Bay Packers, and Cleveland Browns. But we're not going to concede anything. We will play to win every week. I'll demand it. Our fans deserve nothing less.

The people of Jacksonville have been tremendous. We have sold out every home game through the 1997 season, which gives you some idea of our fan support. This is a great football area, and it waited a long time for an NFL franchise.

No matter what happens in the years ahead, I'll never forget the first year we spent in Jacksonville, putting the dream known as the Jaguars together. We watched as the Gator Bowl was razed to the ground and rebuilt with a seating capacity of seventy-three thousand at a total cost of $121 million.

Working in our trailer, we could feel the vibration of the jackhammers and heavy equipment in the stadium. Sometimes I'd go out to watch the construction. It reminded me of the *Star Wars* movies with all the haze in the air. There was almost a glow to the place. Tractors were rolling by, and concrete slabs were swinging on overhead cranes.

It was a different world, and I liked it because it kept me in touch with what we were doing, which was building a football team.

When I'd step outside, the dust from the stadium would blow in my face and one of the workers would shout, "How's it going, coach?" It put things in perspective for me. I'd get to the office at 6:00 A.M. and see the crew already hard at work inside the stadium, and it gave me a sense of urgency.

One of the highlights of 1994 was the signing of our first ten players on December 15. All ten were young players with some NFL experience. The night before they were introduced to the media, we had a welcoming dinner at which our coaches and the new players shared a champagne toast.

I'm not normally an emotional person, but I was emotional that night. Looking around the room, finally having players to coach after almost a full year of waiting, I felt tremendous pride. I told each guy in the room that he was special and that I wanted him to feel that way.

The next day the players were introduced, and each was presented a key to the city by Jacksonville's mayor, Ed Austin.

The most critical part of my job as head coach is to identify talent and find the players who best fill our needs. If we are to be competitive with the other NFL teams, we cannot afford to have made mistakes in this area.

I'll try to explain what the building process was like for our football team and perhaps help those who are faced with starting a business of their own. It is a huge task to combine all the responsibilities that come with the regular job — in my case, head coach — with the added concern of new facilities, new staff, new market, new everything.

Try not to think about how formidable your workload is. It seems as though there aren't enough hours in the day to get everything done. With a new team or company, you step in to a situation in which you're not only the head coach or boss, but part-designer, part-engineer, and full-time visionary.

There is no such thing as a typical day. One morning may be spent going over blueprints with the engineers, figuring out the best location for a practice field. The next morning you may be interviewing applicants for the job of film director, assistant trainer, or ball boy. The next morning it will be something else entirely different.

I found there are two keys to dealing with this situation. First, don't try to do everything yourself. Launching an enterprise such as an NFL franchise involves a great many business issues, including ticket sales, promotions, marketing, community relations, and so on.

With the Jaguars, our principal owner Wayne Weaver brought in an experienced staff of businesspeople to handle those matters, so I didn't have to get deeply involved. I spent virtually all my time overseeing the football operation. Most entrepreneurs are not as fortunate.

The second key is to organize your time. If you thought you were organized before, you have to be doubly organized now because you must make room for more staff meetings and more odds and ends. Things I once took for granted, such as having enough kicking tees for practice, had to be addressed. With a new team or business, there are a million details — and they all must be checked and double-checked.

An important element in achieving success in any business

is surrounding yourself with capable, hard-working people. It is particularly important when you are starting a new venture because there is twice as much work to do, and you have only each other to lean on.

One of the first things I did after accepting the job with the Jaguars was hire six men who had worked with me at Boston College: receivers coach Pete Carmichael, secondary coach Randy Edsall, running backs coach Jerald Ingram, line coach Mike Maser, and linebackers coach Steve Szabo. I also hired Fran Foley, our recruiting coordinator, to work in the personnel department.

I knew from experience that I could work with these guys. I knew them, and they knew me. It was a great help because we could dive into our work. We didn't have to waste a lot of time getting acquainted.

Because of the big job at hand, I wanted people around me who had a tremendous work ethic. I knew what I was getting with these six guys. They had no NFL experience, but that did not concern me. Their work ethic is second to none, and that was more important. Experience, you gain with time.

The five coaches, plus Foley, joined me in Jacksonville in February 1994. We spent the first year traveling the country, scouting college and pro talent. By the time the football season ended, we had detailed evaluations on all twenty-eight NFL teams, plus the top college players who were coming out in the draft.

We really did our homework. Even though we didn't have any games to prepare for, my staff actually put together three game plans during the season. We met as a staff and planned for an opponent just as we would if we had a game that week. Because we didn't have any players, we prepared game plans by system, matching what we saw as our system against another team's system. We put in plays, blitzes — a whole package. It helped keep us sharp as a staff and also kept us from going stir crazy at a time when we had no real games to play.

After the 1994 season ended, I filled out my staff by hiring six coaches who had worked in the NFL that season. They included my coordinators, Kevin Gilbride on offense and Dick Jauron on defense. Kevin worked in Houston for six years, and Dick was in Green Bay for nine seasons.

I wasn't working on a quota system — five coaches the first year, six more coaches the second year — I did what felt right to me. I wanted initially to have a solid group in place in 1994, which we had. Then, we added another group of coaches, fresh off an NFL season, who provided insights on trends and players.

I was looking for a good blend, which is what we achieved. I didn't want a staff of retreads — a bunch of coaches who had knocked around the league for twenty-five years, going from team to team. I wanted coaches with fresh ideas and a lot of enthusiasm.

I wasn't afraid to start my staff with five coaches who had no pro experience. I knew they were creative guys with good ideas. Ingram and Edsall both are quite young — in their thirties — but I saw that as a plus. They brought an energy and hustle to the job that is infectious.

One thing I didn't like in my time as an NFL assistant coach was the number of coaches I found who were stuck in their ways. Some coaches say, "This is the NFL, and this is the way we do it."

Baloney. That's not the only way to do it. There are many different ways to do almost everything, and part of the excitement of coaching is exploring those different options and finding the right ones.

I knew if I ever became a head coach in the NFL, I would put together a staff that would generate new ideas, and not just because new ideas fit nicely with a new team. New ideas can win games and put you ahead of the pack. That is what we were aiming for.

As the head coach of an expansion team, I spend a lot of time studying personnel. Veteran teams have the luxury of a stable roster. Once they make the final squad cut in September, most of those teams don't change much during the season.

By contrast, we will be looking to upgrade every chance

we get. Every time a player is waived by another team, we will ask, "Is he better than what we have at that position?" If he is, we'll bring him in.

We expect a great deal of turnover on our roster in our first couple of seasons. Every NFL expansion team goes through the same thing. Turnover makes it difficult to develop continuity on the team with players coming and going; but as head coach, your primary job is to improve the talent level. Talent still is what wins in this league.

Before we look too far into the future, let's backtrack for a moment. Let me go back to January 1994 and explain how I made the decision to leave a great job as head coach at Boston College to take on the challenge of an NFL expansion team.

Just one year earlier I had turned down an offer to coach the New York Giants in order to stay at Boston College. As it turned out, Dan Reeves took the New York job and led the team to the NFC playoffs in his first year.

So the question is, Why would I turn down a head-coach job with the Giants, after having won a Super Bowl ring as an assistant coach with them in 1990, and then take a job with the Jaguars, a team with no players, no coaching staff, and a trailer for an office?

The whole thing was a matter of timing. The Giants' offer, attractive as it was, came at the wrong time for me. The Jaguars' offer came at what I felt was the right time, so I explored it thoroughly and accepted. I am confident I made the right decision.

The Giants approached me after the 1992 season, my second season as head coach at Boston College. Our team had improved from 4–7 in 1991 to 8–3–1 in 1992, which on paper looks like great progress. But I was disappointed.

We were unbeaten in 1992 after eight games (7–0–1) and really in position to do great things. We had beaten Penn State for only the second time in school history, and the program appeared to be taking off. But our players did not handle the success very well; I blame myself for that.

The kids seemed to let down after the win at Penn State. We

coasted past Tulane and Temple, then we got killed by Notre Dame, 54–7. The next week we lost, 27–10, at home to Syracuse in what I felt was a ho-hum effort by our whole squad.

Still, we got a bid to the Hall of Fame Bowl, which should have engergized the team. But, instead of bouncing back, we got drilled by Tennessee, 38–23. We weren't even competitive in that game.

I was very displeased with the way we finished the season. The program still needed work. We were getting closer but weren't quite there. So when Giants general manager George Young approached me about succeeding Ray Handley as head coach in New York, I said no.

It was not an easy decision. I was born and raised in upstate New York, so coaching the Giants would have been like coming home. I enjoyed my years as an assistant coach with the team and have the utmost respect for Wellington Mara and his family, who own half of the franchise. They all are great people and were wonderful to me.

But I'm the kind of person who cannot walk away from a job when it is half-finished, or even five-eighths finished. When I take on a task, I see it through. I wasn't satisfied with where the football program was at that point. I wasn't about to go anywhere, not even back to the NFL, until that was resolved.

The way the 1993 season began, it appeared the team was going backward. We lost to Miami, 23–7, and to Northwestern, 22–21, in our first two games. Then we regrouped to win eight in a row, including a 41–39 victory at Notre Dame, which was decided by David Gordon's 41-yard field goal on the very last play. It was the most thrilling moment of my coaching career, even greater than winning a Super Bowl with the Giants.

I was very proud of our 1993 squad. We had outstanding leadership from upperclassmen, which allowed us to recover from the 0–2 start. It was a hungrier team than the one from the year before, more mature and focused. The values I wanted to instill in the program finally had taken root. As I watched the team play that season, I could see the growth.

We went to the CarQuest Bowl and whipped a good Virginia team, 31–13. We graduated 100 percent of our seniors that year and brought in the finest recruiting class in the history of the school. All in all, I felt the program was in excellent shape, much further along than the previous year.

So when Jacksonville called me in February, one month after the season ended, I was ready to listen. The timing was right.

Initially, I wasn't sure if this was the best move for me and my family. My wife, Judy, loved Boston College and so did our four children. I finally had the program where I wanted it. Did I really want to leave a sure thing at BC for a leap into the unknown?

I didn't know but was willing to consider it.

I wouldn't have done it if I hadn't had total confidence in the people running the show in Jacksonville. I wanted to be a head coach in the NFL but didn't want it badly enough to take a job that I felt was tied to a less-than-stable ownership.

I arranged to meet with Wayne Weaver, the Jaguars' chairman and chief executive officer, and David Seldin, the club president. For the sake of secrecy, we met at a quiet hotel in Providence, Rhode Island.

We talked for four hours at our first meeting. I interviewed Wayne and David as much as they interviewed me. I wanted to see how committed they were to building a winning team.

I liked both men right from the start. When you are in the business of coaching and recruiting, you learn how to analyze people. I felt good about Wayne and David. They were very forthright, honest, and sincere. They had a solid plan for the franchise. They were enthusiastic but also realistic.

Weaver knows how to build a winner. In 1978 he took over a small women's footwear company that was grossing $9 million a year and turned it into a 200-store chain that grew to $500 million in annual sales. Wayne is an aggressive businessman who gets things done, whether he is selling shoes or selling pro football. He doesn't believe in doing things halfway, and neither do I. That attitude is why we get along.

You have to feel good about the people you work for —

especially when you start a new venture with someone else's capital or under the umbrella of a parent corporation. Things are not going to be smooth when you start a business from the ground up. One thing that will keep you going is your belief in the people on top and their belief in you. But if there is a lack of faith on either side, it won't work.

Weaver and Seldin made it clear that they wanted someone who would take on the dual tasks of head coach and general manager. I said that I preferred to have the final say on football and player-personnel matters.

I gave Wayne and David my assurance that any team I coached would be the best-conditioned, best-prepared, and most highly motivated in the league. I didn't care if it was an expansion team. I would adhere to the same high standards. No one would outwork us. That was a promise.

Judging by the look in Wayne's eye, I could tell he liked that pledge.

By the time we parted that night, I was excited about the possibility of coaching in Jacksonville; and I believe Weaver and Seldin were feeling pretty good about hiring me. Nothing was signed, but we were definitely close.

We met again the next day in Boston for another two and a half hours. Most of the time was spent discussing contract terms and salary. We agreed on a five-year deal and then flew to Jacksonville for the formal announcement.

I gave it a lot of thought, as anyone would. I weighed what I had at Boston College against the opportunity I saw in Jacksonville. You couldn't say one choice was right and the other was wrong. It depends on the individual and his goals.

In my case, I looked at it as a competitor. I said to myself, "If you turn this down, what are you saying about yourself? Are you afraid of a challenge?"

The challenge was what motivated me to put aside my personal feelings for Boston College, which were very deep, to take the job with the Jaguars. I kept thinking this might be my only chance to do something truly historic, to be the original head coach of an NFL franchise. I couldn't pass it up.

One selling point Weaver used in our talks was the enthusiasm of the fans in Jacksonville. He promised the Jaguars would have the most passionate fan support in the NFL. When he told me how the community rallied behind the effort to bring an expansion team to the city, it really got me excited.

Jacksonville had to overcome long odds just to be considered for an NFL franchise. With a population of 656,000 and a television market that ranks fifty-fifth in the United States, it seemed like a small town compared with Baltimore, Memphis, and St. Louis, the other cities in competition for the last available NFL expansion location.

At one point, Jacksonville dropped out when the ownership group and local government could not agree on a lease for the renovated Gator Bowl. A month later the parties got back together and worked things out.

What put the deal over the top was the public response to a ticket drive. The challenge was to sell ten thousand season tickets in ten days, and the team did it. Wayne called the campaign "Ten Days to Glory," and it opened the eyes of club owners and executives around the NFL.

The league awarded the franchise to Jacksonville on November 30, 1993. Within two days, thirty-three thousand more season tickets were sold. It is not surprising when you consider the Jacksonville Bulls were the attendance leader in the now-defunct United States Football League. It is a great football area.

In the summer of 1994 we already had a Jaguars booster club with more than two thousand members. The booster club booked — one year ahead of time — one hundred hotel rooms in Canton, Ohio, for the weekend of our first preseason game, the 1995 Hall of Fame Game.

With such rabid interest, we didn't have to worry, as most new businesses do, about marketing our product. When I do a speaking engagement, I don't have to open by saying, "Hello, I'm Tom Coughlin and this is what I represent . . ."

The people of Jacksonville already know.

Most of them have been waiting their whole lives for a major-league franchise to call their own, and we're it.

From the day I took the job, I had people asking me, "How many games are we gonna win?" or saying, "We'll be in the Super Bowl next year." I just smile and encourage those people because that enthusiasm is a big part of what will drive this team.

We're going to have some tough times, as all expansion teams do, but I really believe the enthusiasm of these fans will not wane. If they see our team playing as hard as it can every week, and management is taking things in the right direction, they will stick with us.

Do Your Homework

As I mentioned earlier, after I took the Jaguars job I sought out Tom Landry and John McKay for guidance. Just because you are starting a new team doesn't mean you have to start with zero background. I've always believed in doing my homework.

Landry and McKay each had an excellent perspective on expansion teams, having coached them in the past. Both men are outstanding coaches — Landry is in the Pro Football Hall of Fame — but neither won a game in his first NFL season.

It doesn't get much worse than that. Yet each coach managed to build his team into a winner. In Landry's seventh season in Dallas, the Cowboys went to the NFL Championship Game. In 1972 they won their first Super Bowl. Over the years, the Cowboys were so successful and so popular that they became known as "America's Team."

The Buccaneers made it to the top in a hurry but, unlike the Cowboys, were not able to stay there. Under McKay Tampa Bay made the playoffs in its fourth season, 1979. They went to the NFC Championship Game but lost, 9–0, to the Los Angeles Rams. If the Buccaneers had won that game, they would have been in Super Bowl XIV against Pittsburgh.

Tampa Bay also had winning seasons in 1981 and 1982, but the team has fallen on hard times since then. The Buccaneers have lost ten games or more in each of the last twelve seasons and have gone through four head coaches since McKay left after the 1984 season.

Landry and McKay both offered me good advice. They stressed the need for patience. When you come from winning programs as they did — Landry had been an assistant coach with the Giants, McKay had been head coach at USC — you become accustomed to things working a certain way. You have good players and good morale, which adds up to a winning attitude.

With an expansion team or a budding enterprise, it is a constant struggle. It is hard to win one game, much less two in a row. There always are a lot of changes on the roster, so it is difficult to build team chemistry. As head coach, you have to be patient and resilient.

When I talked to Landry, he said it was going to be tough. He said it was his faith in himself and his coaching ability that carried him through the first five seasons in Dallas when the Cowboys won only eighteen games and lost forty-six. He said he had his low points, as anyone would, but never got totally sidetracked. He never came close to giving up.

Landry also said something that made a lasting impression on me. He said with a new team, it is vital that the head coach have a solid commitment from the owner. The head coach has to make the owner see the big picture: that while he may not be winning games right away, he is assembling the pieces of what will be a winning team in the near future.

Landry did that with Clint Murchison, the original Cowboys owner. By 1963 the team had a quality quarterback in Don Meredith, an all-pro halfback in Don Perkins, and a future Hall of Fame defensive lineman in Bob Lilly. The foundation was in place. All Landry needed was a little more time.

Murchison realized that and supported Landry even as many in Dallas called for the coach's dismissal.

Landry said he believed the turning point for the franchise

came in February 1964. The Cowboys were coming off a 4–10 season, and there was speculation that Landry was on his way out.

Murchison called a press conference and announced he was giving his head coach a ten-year contract. That ended all the talk about Landry's future and gave the franchise a sense of stability, which is exactly what it needed.

In 1966 the Cowboys started a run of eight consecutive seasons in the playoffs, a streak that reached eighteen playoff appearances in twenty years, all under Landry. He took the team to five Super Bowls. Having watched Landry for years and having coached against him, I admire him tremendously. He is a real pro, a coach's coach.

Define Roles

In our conversation Landry spoke about the importance of defining roles, especially in a new organization. Some new businesses hire people without a clear idea of where they will fit in.

"We'll figure it out," they say.

Well, they may figure it out and they may not. But the point is, in the meantime, the organization is not operating as efficiently as it could. You cannot afford to waste time, especially when you are a new business and are already playing catch-up with the competition. If anything, you have to be more efficient than the other guys.

The Cowboys did that very well. When Murchison built the original team, he put Landry in charge of the football operation and put general manager Tex Schramm, a bright man with experience in public relations and television, in charge of the business office. The team brought in a third man, Gil Brandt, to head the scouting department.

Each person understood his responsibilities and took care of them. It took a while, but when they finally built a winning team, it was built to last — because there was continuity in the organization. The owner was not panicking and changing the staff every year. The players would change, but management held steady.

Landry, Schramm, and Brandt knew they had the full support of ownership, so they were able to build the team the right way rather than build for the quick fix. When an owner or owners are impatient and go into a cycle of firing head coaches and general managers every year or two, they usually create more problems than they solve.

So I'm confident about our franchise in Jacksonville. Weaver and Seldin understand that building this team is the ultimate challenge and that the only way we can succeed is if we tackle it together. Ours is going to be a team effort, from top to bottom.

I studied how the various expansion teams had been built. Some went with older players in hopes of winning right away. Others went with young players, building for the future. My opinion is that you need a mix. A few experienced players provide leadership, but I want mostly young players who have a chance to grow with the program.

McKay was very frank. He warned me not to put much stock in the veteran players who were made available in the January 1995 expansion draft. Each of the twenty-eight established teams had to put six players in a pool. The two new teams, the Panthers and the Jaguars, were able to draft a minimum of thirty players apiece from the pool.

There were some big names on the list of available players, including Michael Dean Perry, the all-pro defensive tackle from Cleveland, and Chris Doleman, a defensive end from Atlanta who once led the league in sacks. The trouble was that each player was on the list for a reason. He was either coming off an injury, slowing down with age, or — in Perry's case — making too much money.

We had to be very careful in making our selections. While I would have liked to draft Perry, we could not afford his $3.2 million salary. Like all NFL teams, we must operate within a salary cap of $36 million. With so many needs, we could not tie up such a big chunk of that money in any one player. Most businesses haven't got the salary cap handicap. But they do have budgets, and the same caution about paying one employee too much probably applies.

There was no salary cap in 1976 when the Buccaneers came into the league, but McKay still found the veteran draft largely a waste. Most of the players he selected were gone within a year. His advice to me was to go for youth, build through the college draft, and focus on defense. "A good defense will keep you in every game," he said.

With more veteran players available to us, and the league allowing us to pick one-two at the top of each round in the college draft, plus getting extra picks in each of the seven rounds, some people predicted the two expansion teams would be competitive with the other clubs right away.

In fact, during the expansion draft in February, former 49ers head coach Bill Walsh said on TV that the Jaguars had better talent than some established NFL teams and, with free agency help, could win six games in the 1995 season. We hadn't even held a minicamp yet, and already expectations were pretty high.

Too many people overstated the situation. Yes, as Walsh said, there was one means of player procurement available to Carolina and Jacksonville that was not available to past expansion teams — free agency. But that did not automatically mean it would be easier for us to build a winning team.

The top free agents are anything but free. Look at Reggie White in Green Bay. He's a great player, and you'd love to have him, but he cost the Packers $4.2 million a year. Ken Harvey is a terrific linebacker who left Phoenix in 1994 and signed with Washington. Technically, he is a free agent, but the Redskins paid $2.7 million to sign him.

There were a lot of good players on the open market again in 1995, guys who could have helped our team, but we couldn't spend the money to sign them — not when we had fifty-three roster spots to fill and only $36 million to spend. It did not make sense to tie up a huge chunk of money in one big-name player and leave ourselves short in four other areas.

We felt the smart way to go was to spread the money around and fill as many holes as possible. So while there is free agency, it wasn't the great advantage to us that some people would have had you believe.

As McKay predicted, the list of available veterans had few surprises. Guys coming off injuries, guys with high salaries, and guys who were a little too small or too slow. There weren't many offensive or defensive linemen, and there weren't *any* Walter Paytons.

We had the first pick in the expansion draft and selected Steve Beuerlein, a solid veteran quarterback who won a Super Bowl ring as a backup to Troy Aikman in Dallas. Beuerlein had a very good season as a starter with the Cardinals in 1993 but lost his job when Buddy Ryan took over as head coach the following year. Ryan chose not to protect Beuerlein in the draft, so we grabbed him.

To me, the key players on any team are the quarterback on offense and the people who pressure the quarterback on defense. With Beuerlein we felt we had a capable player to run our offense. We used the college draft to build the defense.

We will be a young team, a team with a future and potential for growth. I feel we have an edge in attracting undrafted college free agents because we put a premium on youth. A kid who might get lost in the shuffle in Dallas or San Francisco will get a better look and chance to grow with our team.

The first ten players we signed, the ones we greeted with a champagne toast, had an average age of twenty-four. We also went young in the expansion draft. The oldest player we selected was Beuerlein, who is thirty, and that is not old for a quarterback.

An expansion team is pro football's land of opportunity. That is how we presented it to the players we drafted and signed. We said, "Hey, whatever you have to offer, you'll have a chance to display it here." I think that's an angle that also would work for a new business.

We brought in some players who were once highly touted prospects and, for whatever reason, failed to deliver. Two are former Heisman Trophy winners: quarterback Andre Ware, who was released by Detroit and Minnesota, and flanker Desmond Howard, who did not live up to expectations in Washington.

We also picked up two other players who had been first-round draft picks in 1992: offensive tackle Eugene Chung (New England) and tight end Derek Brown (Giants). Like Ware and Howard, these are players with great ability. It is our hope they will see Jacksonville as a fresh start.

I worked out Ware myself. He showed great arm strength and he ran the 40-yard dash in 4.65 seconds, which is excellent for a quarterback. This is a guy who set twenty-six NCAA records and threw seventy-five touchdown passes in only twenty-seven games at the University of Houston. The Lions drafted him in 1990, but he was stuck behind Erik Kramer and Rodney Peete and started only six games in four years.

When we signed him, Andre told me, "This is a starting over point for me." He seemed committed to proving he can play at this level.

I'm counting on those qualities — desire, determination, wanting to prove something — to help us, especially in the first year. I've looked for players who have that attitude.

I didn't want players who, regardless of their ability, would look upon playing for an expansion team as a sentence. I knew quite a few veteran players would. That's why signing free agents was even harder for us, even though we had the money under our salary cap to be a competitive bidder.

Many free agents wanted to sign with teams that had a shot at winning the Super Bowl. Deion Sanders, Ricky Jackson, and Richard Dent did that in the 1994 season, signing with San Francisco, and it worked out for them. Other players decided that's what they wanted, too.

That wish to be on a winner immediately only makes our job as an expansion team tougher. We have to sell the players an entirely different package, and I know it's not for everyone.

We have to sell players on the challenge, the chance to be a part of history, the chance to be a pioneer with a new team.

We have to sell the enthusiasm of the Jacksonville community and the tremendous fan support.

Those were all the things that excited me about going to Jacksonville, but it takes a certain kind of person. You must have mental toughness. You can't be afraid to venture into the unknown. Signing with the Jaguars required a certain leap of faith, and many players would sooner take a sure thing. To play for our team, you have to be highly motivated.

Make No Excuses

It is important in any new business venture that, as the owner, head coach, or CEO, you don't build in excuses for failure. You don't want to create a work environment that says, "We're new, so we don't have to be good."

That is just another way of saying you don't want to work very hard. And that is a cop-out.

If you are a professional, and you are charging people full price for a ticket, you owe them a major-league product. I'm not naive: I know we aren't going to win a division title our first year, but our players are going to be prepared, mentally and physically, for every game. We're going to give people their money's worth.

My approach is to challenge our players. Our playbook and locker room are full of references to "The fastest expansion team to . . ." We break it down line by line.

Fastest expansion team to win five games.

Fastest expansion team to reach .500.

Fastest expansion team to make the playoffs.

We put it out there for our coaches and players to see and to help them set their sights accordingly. We're running a race against history. We want to reach those milestones faster than any previous expansion team. That is our goal.

I'm a coach who stresses discipline and order. I'm tough on my players and make no apologies for it. When I took over at Boston College, a few kids quit the team rather than pay the price. I was sorry they felt that way, but I wasn't going to change my approach. And I won't change my approach with the Jaguars.

Just because we're an expansion team and no one expects us to win a Super Bowl in our first season doesn't mean that we will run a lazy-man's training camp. I'll work this team just as hard as the others, maybe harder, because it is the only way to instill the good work habits that are the key to winning.

I'm sure our progress will be measured against that of the other expansion franchise, Charlotte. The Panthers took a different course for their start-up. They hired a front office early but did not hire a coaching staff until after the 1994 NFL season was over. They brought in Dom Capers as head coach in January 1995. Previously, he had been the defensive coordinator in Pittsburgh.

Does that mean we are ahead of the Panthers because I spent all of 1994 on the job, scouting players and making plans? I don't know. I feel it is an advantage to have had more time on the job; I have a good handle on what we're doing. But until we play enough games, it is all speculation.

The Panthers have a very experienced front office. Their owner is Jerry Richardson, who was a receiver with the Baltimore Colts and is the only NFL owner to have actually played in the league. Their president, Mike McCormack, was a Hall of Fame tackle with Cleveland and an NFL coach for twenty years. The general manager is Bill Polian, who helped build an AFC championship team in Buffalo.

We have less football experience in our front office. However, we have a solid group of businesspeople assembled by Wayne Weaver, who knows how to put an organization together. We don't have a general manager, so I'm responsible for the football decisions. I'm comfortable with that role because I have an excellent group of assistant coaches and scouts backing me up.

Whenever I feel a bit overwhelmed here, I think back to 1970 when I was hired as head football coach at Rochester (New York) Institute of Technology. I was twenty-two years old and just one year out of Syracuse, where I had played in the same backfield as future NFL greats Larry Csonka and Floyd Little.

At the time, Rochester Tech was playing club football, but there were plans to make it a varsity sport. I was brought in to lay the groundwork. I was a one-man staff: coaching the team, making travel plans, calling hotels to order the pregame meal, fixing the equipment.

I had a few assistant coaches, and we literally did everything from lining the field to assembling the blocking sleds to washing the laundry after practice. We didn't think anything of it; we just did it.

I remember one Saturday when we were playing a home game. At 11:00 A.M., while the players were getting dressed, my coaches and I were pounding fence posts into the ground around the field. The other team pulled up in its bus. The coaches got off in their jackets and ties and looked at us as though we were crazy.

We kept on working until the job was done, then we put the sledgehammers away, changed into our coaching clothes, and did the pregame chalk talk. We won the game, too. I remember that most of all.

I worked at Rochester Tech for four years and was the only winning coach the school ever had. While I was there, I never thought I was wasting my time. It may have been only a club football team, but it was *my* club football team; and that made it the most important team in the world. I gave it my all.

I will do the same in Jacksonville.

Maintaining Perspective

Bud Grant

HEAD COACH

MINNESOTA VIKINGS, 1967—83, 1985

Harold (Bud) Grant seemed the perfect coach for the Minnesota Vikings. Outwardly he appeared as cold as the December winds that swept through old Metropolitan Stadium and sent visiting teams into shivering retreat.

Grant's eyes never left the field, yet his face betrayed no emotion. Jim Murray of the *Los Angeles Times* wrote: "If you came into a game late, it was impossible to tell from looking at Grant whether he was ten points ahead or thirty behind."

Stoic, dispassionate, unemotional. Those were some of the words used to describe Grant in his eighteen seasons as coach of the Vikings. But the people who know him best — his assistant coaches, players, and team staffers — say he was quite the opposite.

"He's the supposed iceberg who sort of boils underneath," says John Michels, who coached the offensive line under Grant. "He enjoys a laugh better than anyone else I know. He is one of the finest people I've ever met. He treats everyone with dignity and respect. That's why players loved playing for him."

In his coaching days, Grant was a quiet man and a stickler for doing things a certain way. For example, he insisted that each player stand at attention during the national anthem with his helmet under the same arm.

But he is not, as some people believe, carved from a glacier. He is quite the opposite; he wept openly when he was inducted into the Pro Football Hall of Fame in 1994.

Grant has a sharp mind and a wry sense of humor. When a club secretary opened her desk on April Fools' Day to find a salamander slithering among the paper clips, she knew immediately whom to blame. Not the ball boys, but the head coach.

Grant set his course in life after growing up in Superior, Wisconsin. He was a three-sport athlete at the University of Minnesota, earning three letters each in football, basketball, and baseball. He played two years of professional basketball with the Minneapolis Lakers; quit to join the NFL's Philadelphia Eagles in 1951; then left after two seasons as an offensive and defensive end to sign with Winnipeg of the Canadian Football League.

Grant was named Winnipeg's head coach in 1957 at age thirty. After winning four CFL championships, he returned to the NFL as head coach of the Vikings in 1967. His record in Minnesota was 168–108–5 (including postseason), with eleven division titles and four Super Bowl appearances in thirteen seasons.

He was not flashy, nor were his teams. But, like him, they were strong, deep, and well-disciplined. He retired after the 1983 season but was coaxed back for one more year in 1985 before leaving coaching for good at age fifty-eight.

Grant loved the game, yet never let it consume him. He always found time for his wife, Pat, and their six children. He once was thirty minutes late for a press conference because his son's high-school basketball game went into double overtime. An avid outdoorsman, he decorated his office with wildlife art and installed a deer feeder near the Vikings' practice field, in view of his office window.

"Bud has more leadership ability and more common sense than any person I've ever been around in my life," says Pro Football Hall of Fame quarterback Fran Tarkenton, who played on

Grant's teams for seven seasons. "He certainly was one of the very few great coaches in our game."

"Bud possessed great leadership and great intuition," adds Fred Zamberletti, the Vikings' longtime trainer. "If I were lost in the north woods in subzero weather and needed one man to lead me to survival, Bud Grant would be my choice."

I played and coached pro football in the United States and Canada for more than thirty years. I honestly can say in all that time I never felt it was a strain.

People talk about the pressure of playing in championship games. I was in a lot of championship games, including four Super Bowls. But I never felt the pressure. Preseason game or championship game, it is still just a game; and no game is a matter of life and death.

I've always tried to keep my work and my life in perspective. As in any business, there is a premium placed on success. In football it is winning. In business it is improving the bottom line. But it is a competitive thing, and there always are people trying to get ahead of you. Still, you should not let it control your life.

That does not mean conceding anything to the competition. In Minnesota our teams won eleven NFL or NFC Central Division titles. We were a dominant football team. But I assure you, no one on those teams — coaches, players, trainers, anyone — experienced burnout. We won without being obsessive. It isn't that hard to do.

All it takes is organization and discipline, knowing how to get the maximum out of your people in an allotted time. Plan ahead; know what you want to do; then set up a schedule and stick with it.

When your work is done, go home and do something else. It's a long season — or career. Don't make it longer.

I had a routine I followed for years. I got up at 5:00 A.M. and drove to a duck blind that was halfway between my home and the office. The sun usually was up by six. I could hunt until 7:45 and still get to the office, clean up, and be ready for the 9:00 A.M. coaches' meeting. I was wide awake, my head was clear, and I was ready to dive into football.

I'm not saying everyone should buy a shotgun and head for the nearest duck blind. But some sort of morning ritual, apart from your job, is a healthy thing. Ride a bike; row a boat; walk your dog. While you are waking up, you can think through the day ahead.

With the Vikings we worked hard, putting in the game plan and running the daily practice. But by 6:00 P.M. the coaches usually were on their way home.

I made it a point to have dinner with my wife, Pat, and our six children almost every night. I would not deprive myself of that time. If one of my children had a basketball game or a music recital, I was there.

I hear about coaches who sleep in the office and seldom see their families during the season. I could never do that. What's more, I don't feel it is necessary — in pro football or in any business.

When you are the man in charge, it is easy to let your work devour you. I know some coaches who if you took away football would have nothing. Football is their whole life. It is their vocation, their avocation, their passion, their hobby — everything.

Well, it wasn't mine.

I love football, but I also love my family and the outdoors. Football was my livelihood, so I certainly gave it my best effort, but not to the exclusion of everything else. If you lose the balance in your life, if you sacrifice everything for career, you lose in the long run. I really believe that.

Burnout Is Self-Imposed

I'd like to comment on the "burnout" syndrome. I think burnout is self-imposed. You can work hard without burning out. I worked hard and won a lot of games, but I never burned out. To me, it was just a matter of common sense.

People burn out not because they are doing too much but because they are putting in huge amounts of time without accomplishing anything. Time does not represent work. It is an old axiom, but it is true in all businesses, including football.

There are a couple of traps you can fall into, as a coach and as a company executive. One of them is becoming so reliant on technology that you get bogged down in it and ultimately are less efficient. I saw it in the latter days of my coaching career when every team in the NFL, including the Vikings, began using computers.

On one hand, the computer simplified things, which was good. But on the other hand, it meant you could do more things in terms of charting other teams' tendencies. As coaches, we found much of what we did in those areas was redundant. We overdid it just because it was there.

If you look in a typical office, you'll see the same thing: people at computers doing work that someone else did an hour before, but they don't realize it.

The increased emphasis on watching game and practice film was another example. Almost every team in the league now videotapes its practices and studies the tape each day. I didn't do that.

As head coach, I could see most of what went on during a practice. I had a good feel for what was working and what wasn't working and why. I did not need to chart every down and distance situation, document every play, and go back and check it against the film.

I think sometimes we become so enamored with technology that we get away from the basic skills that made us successful in the first place. For me, that was my ability to coach by deduction, by feel.

The other trap to avoid is looking back and second-guessing your decisions. That trap is especially dangerous for a football coach.

Football is a forward-looking business. What happened in

the last game is only important on Monday, the day after the game. As a coach, you analyze it, learn from it, and then bury it.

You cannot second-guess yourself. Make decisions and then live with them. Remember: your decisions will not be right 100 percent of the time. You need to be right a high percentage of the time, obviously, but no one expects you to be right all the time. So don't let your mistakes eat you alive.

That's why coaches wind up taking Maalox for breakfast. I never did that, and it wasn't because I was not competitive. I'm every bit as competitive as Mike Ditka, Jimmy Johnson, or any other coach you can name. I'd do anything and everything within the rules to win a game; but if it wasn't enough on a given day, I could accept that.

There is no disgrace in saying, "We did the best we could." As a coach, you cannot ask more from a player or yourself.

Football is a strange game. It is played with a funny-shaped ball, which bounces a lot of ways. As a head coach, you only work on the things you can control. You cannot control the bounce of the ball, the officials, or the weather.

You also have to give the other team credit because those guys have talent and are being paid millions of dollars; sometimes they are going to make plays and beat you. That is part of any sport.

If you're going to be successful in this business, or any business where the stakes are high, you've got to be able to handle losing. We all can handle winning; but if you can't handle losing, it's pretty tough to last in pro sports.

There were nights after games when I tossed and turned, thinking about a play that went wrong or a ball that should have been caught but wasn't. By the next day, however, I was looking ahead to the next game. After a Super Bowl loss I was looking ahead to the next season. One restless night was my limit. If it stays with you more than two nights, then you have to ask the question "Am I in the right business?"

Take the Long View

Obviously, what I am saying here is that you should not overdo it, emotionally or physically. The temptation is there because we're so competitive and the NFL is such a fishbowl world, where everything you do is heavily scrutinized.

But I always thought there was a limit to how hard you could push and how much you could squeeze out of an individual, whether he was a player or a coach. That belief was why I approached rituals such as training camp differently than most coaches.

During my years with the Vikings, we had the shortest training camps of any NFL team. I would bring the team to camp seven days before our first preseason game. Other teams would be in a camp for weeks before our players even reported.

During our camps there was a minimum of hitting and very little scrimmaging. Other teams hit twice a day, every day, for six weeks. They got a lot of players injured in the process. I did not see the point.

The main asset of any team is the players. It is not the coaches, the equipment, the office staff, or the physical plant.

The players are the number-one asset, which means the coach's most important job is choosing the right players and seeing to it they are ready for the regular season. Not the first preseason game, or the fourth, but the regular season that begins in September and runs through December. It is a long grind and requires a long view on the part of the man in charge.

One reason we were able to spend less time in training camp was that we did not bring as many players to camp as other teams. Some teams brought 125 players to camp. We never brought more than seventy.

Why? Because I did not want to waste time on players who could not compete at the NFL level. I ran a training camp, not a tryout camp. I didn't care about providing opportunities for free agents. I was concerned with one thing: putting a team together.

With our small group, I knew who the players were after three days. We settled on the forty or fifty guys we were going with and spent the rest of the preseason molding them into a unit.

I heard about other teams that brought in these cattle calls of 100 to 130 players, with fifty or sixty free agents. They would spend — waste, really — the first month cutting away the deadwood. They would spend the preseason evaluating players they were not going to keep, instead of coaching the players they *were* going to keep.

To me, that seemed backward.

We would have staff meetings in which I'd have exchanges with my assistant coaches that went like this:

"Can this guy play?"

"Well, he is six-four and runs pretty well."

"But can he play?"

"He's kind of raw."

"Can he play?"

"Not really."

"Then get him out of here."

I valued my coaches too much to have them wasting time with guys who did not belong in an NFL camp. If we spent two hours on the practice field, I wanted my coaches spending that time with players who were going to be with us all season.

Why coach a guy that you know darn well is going to be gone in three or four days? It doesn't make sense.

Why do other teams insist on doing that? I think it's a comfort factor. There is an old expression: strength in numbers. To some football coaches, there is comfort in numbers. They see 120 players on a practice field and think, "There has to be a team in there somewhere."

Also it probably looks good to the owner and front office to have all these players around. There is a lot of scrimmaging and a lot of film to watch, and a head coach can say, "Look at how busy I am."

There was a big push toward this sort of thing in the 1970s because Dallas and Washington were having some success with free agents, and other teams were quick to imitate. I stuck with what I knew worked for me.

In business there is a similar mentality. Some company adds nine vice-presidents and launches a dozen satellite operations, and there is pressure for other companies in that field to do the same thing. But if you had success the other way, being lean and mean, it is a mistake to change. Why play catch-up if you aren't behind?

It is absolutely critical that your superiors understand what you are doing and why. I was lucky in Minnesota because my superiors were owner Max Winter and general manager Jim Finks, both of whom understood sports. Winter once owned the NBA Lakers, and Finks was an NFL quarterback with Pittsburgh and a coach at Notre Dame before he moved into management.

Winter and Finks both were very comfortable with my approach to training camp and football in general. They saw the value in what we were doing as a team. The fact that we won consistently was the bottom line.

Of course, if I worked for two people who didn't really know the game, they may have looked at our small training camps and asked, "Why don't we do things like George Allen? He brings a lot more players to camp."

I never had to contend with that sort of thing, which is why I stayed on the job in Minnesota for eighteen years.

Make the Playbook Fit the Players

One of the great challenges of coaching, or any management position, is adapting to change and adapting correctly. You must recognize when it is time to try something else, and you must have the right answer to what that something else should be.

As a football coach, you must learn to adapt to your personnel. We went through several phases with the Vikings and won championships with all of them.

It started in the late 1960s when we had a strong running attack with Dave Osborn and Bill Brown carrying the ball. Later we got Fran Tarkenton to play quarterback and drafted Chuck Foreman, a halfback who could catch like a wide receiver, so we went to a short-passing game.

We took on another look with Ahmad Rashad and Sammy White as wide receivers. They had the speed to go deep, so we became more of a big-play passing offense.

Three very different looks, but each one got us to a Super Bowl.

I always felt that, as a head coach, you have to work with what you have and build a system that fits the personnel. I think the biggest mistake a coach can make is to hang on to the same playbook for thirty years and try to fit each and every player in a predetermined role.

Some guys do certain things better than others, so why not use that to your advantage? It would have been silly for me to make Foreman run the same plays as Osborn, and vice versa.

You need a basic operating framework, such as our camps and our practices, that stays pretty much unchanged. But within that framework, you constantly have to adjust and fine-tune because the game does evolve.

In business I suppose the correlation would be asking your salespeople to follow the same handbook they followed in the 1950s. You are not going to win by having your people sell brushes door-to-door while the competition is using the Home Shopping Channel. You have to be competitive every day or you lose ground you may never make up.

One thing I really valued as a coach was experience and continuity. To use our 1974 Super Bowl team as an example, we had fourteen players on the roster with ten or more years' NFL experience, spending most of that time with us. Two members of that group were tackle Grady Alderman and defensive end Jim Marshall, who were members of the original Vikings team in 1961.

Having such a large number of veterans on the team allowed me to do some of the things I did. For example, it allowed me to bring the team to training camp later than anyone else, because so many of the players knew the system and knew that it was mandatory to report in good shape, ready to go.

On our teams the veterans did almost as much teaching as the coaches. We had guys, such as linebacker Roy Winston and center Mick Tingelhoff, who knew the defense and offense as well as the coaches did. They could pull a rookie aside on the practice field and explain what the rookie was doing wrong.

That is one of the problems I see in the NFL today, with all the free-agent movement. Teams are experiencing up to 40 percent turnover from one year to the next. That flux makes it hard for a head coach because he almost has to start from scratch each season and teach the ABCs of his system rather than take that system up to the next level.

Handling people is a key element in the success or failure of any coach or executive. To me, this was the simplest part of the equation. Follow one basic rule: Treat people the way you would like to be treated yourself.

I had an advantage when I became a head coach with Winnipeg of the Canadian Football League in 1957. I had played professional sports for years: first semipro baseball, then basketball with the Minneapolis Lakers, and football with the Eagles and Winnipeg.

I played under a number of coaches and, although I was not thinking about a career in coaching at the time, made mental notes on each one. What did this coach do well? What did that coach do wrong?

So when they asked me to hang up my jersey and take over as coach in Winnipeg in 1957, I had a pretty good idea what I wanted to do. My first rule was to treat every player as an equal. I think that approach is very important.

I was a good player and, along the way, received more than my share of preferential treatment. I could make a mistake, and the coach wouldn't say anything. But another player would make the same mistake and get chewed out on the spot.

I never thought that was right.

Ask anyone who ever played for me, and he will tell you that I treated all my players the same way. It didn't matter if you were Chuck Foreman or Joe Blow; if you made a mistake, you heard about it and you knew exactly where you stood. There were no sacred cows, nor were there any scapegoats.

The other thing I learned — and this goes back to my basketball coach at the University of Minnesota — was never to discipline a player in front of his teammates. In business this policy would translate into never criticizing a worker in front of his coworkers.

All it does is embarrass the individual and probably make him resentful, while sending a message to the rest of the group, "Hey, this guy is a foul-up. We can't trust him."

So how can you expect him to perform — and the other players to respond — if he is asked to make a critical play in the next game? It is a negative situation all the way around.

If I had to criticize a player, or settle a difference of opinion, it always was done in the privacy of my office; no one else knew about it. I did not air those things in front of the team and certainly not in the media.

Another trick I learned from my old basketball coach was that if you have something critical to say to a player, preface it by saying something positive. That way, when you get to the criticism, at least you know he will be listening. If you start off blasting a guy, he might just tune you out — and you wind up wasting your breath.

There are some things I did as head coach that would be considered old-fashioned today. For example, I had a small coaching staff. When I took over in Minnesota, I had four assistants. When we went to our first Super Bowl in 1969, I had six assistants.

I thought that was sufficient. I still think that is enough to get the job done, although I look around the NFL now and see that most teams have a dozen assistant coaches, sometimes more. What do they all do?

It seems that in football, or any business, the tendency now is to hire too many people. It might be the comfort factor again. If you have a lot of assistant coaches, or company vice-presidents, you feel like you have all your bases covered. Not necessarily.

I was less concerned with numbers than efficiency. I felt we were more efficient working with a small group of coaches who knew each other well and understood exactly what their responsibilities were. The more people on a staff, the more likely they are to bump into each other.

Put Your Ego Aside

One thing I believe very strongly is that to be a good head coach, or a good administrator, you have to keep your own ego in check. We all have egos — I do, certainly — but your ego cannot be the driving force in your work.

The main job of a coach is to recognize and secure talent, and then to utilize that talent. To do so, the coach has to keep his own personality and ego out of the equation. Make decisions on one basis: can this player help us? If he can, bring him in, whether you like him personally or not.

Coaching is a job, not an ego trip. Coaches or business executives who are wrapped up in their own egos will make decisions on that basis: What's best for me? What reflects the most credit on me?

That is so wrong.

The question should be, What's best for the team?

The celebrity part of the job can warp you. You can become dependent on it, too concerned with who gets the credit, who gets the most time on TV. I tried to keep it all in perspective.

As much as possible, I kept a low profile. It was just easier that way.

My approach to the media was basically to ignore them. My feeling was that winning takes care of everything. A victory said all that needed to be said about my coaching. I did not have to stand up and say, "I did this" and "I did that." Winning was all that mattered, and there was more than enough credit to go around.

The media portrayed me as a cold, unemotional man who never reacted to what happened on the field, good or bad. I was called the "Ice Man" and often was compared to one of the faces on Mount Rushmore.

That isn't me at all — I'm a practical joker, the people in our office will vouch for that. But that was the image the media created for me during my eighteen years of coaching in Minnesota.

I had club officials, guys in the public relations office, come to me and say, "This is terrible. All the press writes about is how you never smile and you don't talk."

I told them not to worry. I wasn't concerned about it, so there was no reason for them to be concerned. It was a stereotype created over the years and was an easy angle for the writer, which I understood.

I didn't care.

I really didn't.

I was a football coach, not a talk-show host. The image I projected on the sidelines — whether I appeared cold, aloof, detached, whatever — was of no concern to me. I was there to do a job, not play to the TV cameras or the fans.

I've kept a newspaper clipping in my desk all these years. It is quote from Chinese philosopher Lao-tzu, in 565 B.C., discussing leadership. It is good advice for any football coach or anyone who is in a position of command:

> A leader is best
> When people barely know he exists.
> Not so good when people obey and acclaim him,

Worse when they despise him.

. . . .

But of a good leader, who talks little,
When his work is done, his aim fulfilled,
They will say, "We did this ourselves."

I really think that's how it should be.

Put your own ego aside. Don't be concerned with people writing about what a great coach you are. Make the team the focus. If the team wins, you have done your job. I did not need any more satisfaction than that.

It amused me that some people mistook my lack of outward emotion for a lack of involvement in the game. Nothing could be further from the truth. I was very involved. I wore a headset and communicated with three different coaches in the booth upstairs. All the offensive and defensive calls went through me. I didn't signal the plays or call them, but I knew what they were. And if I disagreed with one, I said so. Then we would come up with something else.

I tried to stay two or three plays ahead. To do that, you have to concentrate. I could not waste time hollering at officials; hollering at players; or jumping up and down, leading cheers. I was totally immersed in the game.

If that behavior made me appear stoic and unemotional, so be it. I would rather be stoic and in control than animated and out of control, like some coaches I've seen.

Strategy in football can be overrated, and often is, but there really was strategy involved in coaching games at Metropolitan Stadium, which was our home for years before they built the Metrodome in downtown Minneapolis in 1982.

When we played at the old stadium, especially late in the season when the temperature was around zero, I coached according to the conditions. I knew which parts of the field froze first and which parts of the field would start out okay but freeze in the second half. I factored that into our play calling.

The Metrodome is a beautiful facility, and I know it is more comfortable for the fans. But, speaking as a coach, I miss the strategy that was involved in playing in the old stadium in December and January. Moving indoors removes that element from the game.

I don't know if harsh conditions favor one team over another. If the field is frozen, it is frozen for both teams. If the ball is cold and slick, it is cold and slick for both teams.

But we did a good job as a team convincing our opponents that we had a big advantage playing at home in the dead of winter. It was psychological to a large degree. Again, it was a matter of perspective. I didn't make a big deal of the cold, so the players didn't, either.

A sportswriter once wrote: "If you were going to beat the Vikings in the cold in Minnesota, you had to come from Mars." That was just what I wanted our opponents to think. I wanted them to dread coming to our stadium late in the season.

Other teams would come in worrying about the weather, while we concentrated on winning the game. That was our advantage: it wasn't so much the cold as it was our opponents' preoccupation with the cold.

In December 1969 the Rams came to Minneapolis for a playoff game. George Allen, the Rams' coach, was psyched out by the weather. He brought his team to Minneapolis three days early so they could acclimate themselves to the conditions.

It was a ridiculous idea. What can a bunch of guys from California learn in three days in Minnesota? They spent most of the time testing which gloves to wear, which long johns to wear, which heaters to have next to the bench, and so on. They spent 90 percent of their time figuring out how to stay warm and 10 percent of their time looking for ways to beat us.

I eliminated all that. I did not allow our players to wear gloves and did not permit heaters in our bench area. So we had nothing to think about except football.

We won the game, 23–20, on the way to our first Super Bowl.

Over the years many people asked why I insisted on doing

things that way. Some felt I was cruel or foolish — or both — to ban sideline heaters on days when the windchill factor reached thirty degrees below zero. But it seemed to fit my cold, unfeeling image.

To me, it would have been a mistake to make the weather an issue. If I had dwelled on it, the players would have, too. We practiced outdoors every day, so it wasn't like cold weather on Sunday was anything new.

Our players actually looked forward to the games because at least there was a halftime intermission, when they could go inside to have a cup of soup. Practices were two hours straight through, with no break and no cheering fans. The cold always seemed worse on those gray, windy weekdays.

Why no heaters on the sidelines? Because I saw how our opponents huddled around them. A dozen players with their backs to the field, paying no attention to the game and dreading the moment when they would have to go back in.

We did not have heaters, so all our players stood along the sideline — watching the game, cheering and clapping their hands, if only to keep their blood circulating. It gave us a mental edge to have our guys more into the game than our opponents were.

We did not draft our players from the North Pole. We had our share of guys from the West Coast, the Southwest, and the Deep South. They adapted to playing what was known as "Vikings football" and, in fact, took pride in it.

Before games I gave our players a choice: they could take the pregame warmup in their jackets, or they could leave the jackets in the locker room and warm up in their jerseys. It had to be one or the other. I didn't want half the team in jackets and half in jerseys. It had to be uniform.

Without exception, the players voted to go without jackets. Even tackle Ron Yary, who was from USC, and Foreman, who was from Miami, went along. Our players liked to project that rugged image.

The other teams, of course, warmed up in jackets, gloves, hoods, the full arctic-explorer look. Our players came out in their jerseys, and half of them would roll up their sleeves. Bill Brown would stand at midfield in full view of the other team and scrape the scabs off his elbows and let the blood run down his arms.

Our opponents had to think, "These guys are crazy."

Did it help us win those games?

Put it this way: It didn't hurt.

This chapter would not be complete without a discussion of our four Super Bowl appearances, all of which ended in defeat. We lost to Kansas City in Super Bowl IV, 23–7; to Miami in Super Bowl VIII, 24–7; to Pittsburgh in Super Bowl IX, 16–6; and to Oakland in Super Bowl XI, 32–14.

This is where I really have to draw on that word "perspective." I've often been asked about those games. Heck, in some quarters I suppose I've been branded by them. I've heard countless versions of why our team couldn't win "the big one."

We didn't win them, quite simply, because we did not play well enough.

It wasn't a lack of character or resolve. Look at the teams we played: Miami and Pittsburgh were two of the greatest teams of all time, and the Raiders, with that great offensive line, were not far behind. We prepared well and played hard; we just did not win.

That is not a tragedy or a disgrace; it is part of competition.

People who don't know me very well seem to think I am haunted by those four games, that they follow me around like a dark cloud, even today.

That is not true at all.

It is not that I don't care, because — as I've mentioned — I'm as competitive as any coach who ever lived. But looking back on those games, there is nothing I would have changed or anything I would have done differently. We did the best we could. We were beaten by teams that were better on those particular days.

There is anguish in anything if you want to find it; but, to repeat, if you hope to survive in football or any business where the stakes are high, it is absolutely essential to maintain your perspective.

My perspective on all sports, including pro football, is that it is entertainment. I was a football coach, not a brain surgeon or an airline pilot who held people's lives in my hands. I did the best I could and competed to the utmost, but I never lost sight of the fact that it was all entertainment.

I say that, and people seem surprised.

Then I say to them, "Can you tell me who played in the Super Bowl three years ago? Do you remember the score?"

Unless their team was involved or they are sports trivia junkies, they don't remember. So it's like every other form of entertainment; it does not last long.

For me to spend the rest of my days worrying about four football games, or feeling cursed somehow, would be foolish. There are too many other things in life. I have my health and a wonderful family. I was elected to the Pro Football Hall of Fame in 1994. I'm very happy with my life.

I do not think anything in my life would have changed if we had won a Super Bowl. It would have been a great thing for the Vikings' organization, but what would have changed in my life? I doubt that I would have coached any longer than I did. I'd be living in the same house and doing the same things I do today.

It's the same with the Hall of Fame. It was a great honor when I was inducted, a tremendously emotional moment, but being in the Hall of Fame has not changed my life. And if losing four Super Bowls had kept me out of the hall, as many people predicted, that wouldn't have changed my life, either.

I've heard it said the Super Bowl is unfair in the sense that the losing team seldom is given any respect, especially if the team loses more than once. Then it becomes a label.

We went through it, Denver went through it, and Buffalo has gone through it recently. Lose four Super Bowls, and people don't remember the games you won to get there — they only remember the one you lost at the end.

This will surprise you, coming from me, but I never thought much about it. I mean, that is why they call it the Super Bowl. It is winner-take-all, one game. That's why it attracts such a huge audience.

I have no problem with that. Being the best is what our country is based on. It is what made this country stand out from all the other countries in the world — the spirit of competition, striving to be the best. That's what the Super Bowl represents. The winner gets the accolades, and that is how it should be. But I also think the team that loses comes away with something, too.

By striving to be the best, even if you don't quite make it, you make yourself better. You come closer to fulfilling your potential, which should be the goal of each individual.

That is what we preach in America: you can be president; you can be a CEO; you can be a Super Bowl MVP. There is something up there, any one of us can get there, and by striving to get there, even if we fall short, we still reach the top rung of our own abilities.

If you do that, in my opinion, you haven't really lost.

I may have a slightly different view of things because I led a charmed life as an athlete and coach. I often say that my greatest accomplishment is I spent more than thirty years in professional sports and never was cut or fired. Every time I changed teams or changed jobs, it was my call. I don't have any of the scars that other people in this business have. I'm grateful for that.

Most of the great coaches, including even Paul Brown, were fired at one time or another. A few coaches with Super Bowl rings have been fired as well. I see that and realize that winning a Super Bowl isn't always what it is cracked up to be.

I've talked a great deal about how I view football — that is, as a game. A game with tremendous rewards, but still a game. Throughout my coaching career, I tried to impart this to my players, especially the fringe players.

I always felt a player who had marginal ability was wasting his time spending three or four years as a backup, bouncing from team to team. Whenever I released a player like that, I urged him either to go back to school to get his degree, or to take his degree and get on with his life's work.

I would tell him that if he took the work ethic that he applied to football and applied it to another business, he would be much farther ahead than if he left our team and signed with another team for one year, then went to another team the next year.

Some players took my advice; others did not. But I felt better having said it because my conscience was clear. It is gratifying to see some of those men today and see what they've done with their lives. I had a few of them say, "Coach, that was the greatest thing you ever did for me."

Some people have to be told when they are at the end of the road. I knew it instinctively. After the 1983 season I was ready to leave coaching and do other things.

I did not retire because I was tired, drained, or — to borrow that word used by other head coaches — burned out. I did not feel any of that. I never let the game consume me.

I retired because I was fifty-six years old and wanted to do other things while I still had my health. I wanted to travel. I wanted to fish new waters. I wanted to spend more time with my family.

I do not believe you should retire when you are worn out or when you are sick and can't go on any longer. You should retire when the time is right. And for me, the time was right in 1983.

But I wasn't tired of football. Some people assumed that I was, but I wasn't.

I even returned to coach the Minnesota Vikings in 1985, putting my retirement plans on temporary hold. I was asked countless times then if I was coming back to the game "rejuvenated."

My standard reply was, "I never felt 'un-juvenated.' "

I enjoyed my year away from the game and would have stayed retired if Max Winter had not come to me in December 1984 and asked me to come back.

The team had suffered through a 3–13 season in 1984 under my successor, former assistant Les Steckel. It wasn't all his fault. The team had a lot of injuries and Les didn't really get a fair chance to show what he could do. But the season was such a disaster that Winter felt he had to make a change. He asked if I would come back for a year or two and stabilize things while he looked for another head coach.

I took the job on that basis, that it was a short-term thing just to help the team get back on its feet. I did it as a favor to Max and Mike Lynn, the general manager, who treated me so well over the years.

If they felt I could help, fine, I'd give it a try.

The team improved to seven wins in 1985, and I was able to step aside again as Winter and Lynn promoted my long-time assistant Jerry Burns to head coach. Then I retired for the second and final time.

I still have an office at the Vikings' headquarters and am listed on the club directory as a consultant, but it is really an honorary thing. I come and go as I please and stay out of the way as much as possible. Dennis Green is the head coach now, and it is his show.

I don't need to be involved for my ego's sake. I'm satisfied with my career and what I accomplished. I'm quite happy to be free of the day-to-day responsibilities, not that I ever found them overwhelming.

I believe the secret to a happy retirement is not to retire *from* something, but to retire *to* something, which, to me, meant more time at home and more time in the outdoors.

I was thinking about retiring anyway, but the death of the great Alabama head coach Paul (Bear) Bryant the previous January really helped convince me. The Bear retired following the 1982 Liberty Bowl after thirty-eight years in coaching and died one month later.

I thought that was a tragedy.

I told Winter, "I'm fifty-seven, and I still have a lot of things to do. I want time to do them."

One thing I wanted, and this may sound silly, was to see

what August was like. I had spent thirty-six years in professional football. That meant thirty-six training camps, thirty-six Augusts taken up by football. I had no idea what other people did in August. I wanted to find out.

You know what I found? August is a beautiful month. There aren't as many bugs. You can go places, and the mosquitos and wood ticks are almost gone. It is a wonderful time in the garden. I loved it.

If I had not stepped away from football and given myself a chance to enjoy it, I would have missed a lot.

Moving Up from Middle Management

Norv Turner

HEAD COACH

WASHINGTON REDSKINS, 1994—PRESENT

Norval (Norv) Turner was not exactly a household name when Jimmy Johnson hired him as offensive coordinator in Dallas in 1991. Turner was a receivers coach with the Los Angeles Rams at the time, a studious young guy who was in the office every day at 5:00 A.M.

Turner was not Johnson's first choice for the job. The Cowboys' head coach tried, but failed, to land Gary Stevens, an assistant with Miami, and then Ted Tollner, who was with San Diego. He hired Turner, his third choice, on the recommendation of Dave Wannstedt (now head coach of the Chicago Bears), who once worked with Turner at USC.

Quiet and unassuming, Turner did a masterful job of repairing the Dallas offense, which had ranked last in the NFL the previous year. In Turner's first season as offensive coordinator, the Cowboys jumped from twenty-eighth to ninth in total offense and won eleven games en route to the playoffs.

The next year, 1992, Dallas improved to fourth in total offense and second in scoring, with 409 points. Emmitt Smith won the NFL rushing title for the second consecutive year, helping the Cowboys to win the Super Bowl, a feat Dallas repeated in 1993.

For the most part, the Cowboys' offensive personnel did not change in the years 1990 to 1993. Most of the players were the same, including quarterback Troy Aikman and Smith, the MVPs of Dallas's victories in Super Bowls XXVII and XXVIII.

So what made the difference? The players point to Turner, who streamlined the offense and tailored it to fit the talents of Smith, Aikman, and wide receiver Michael Irvin.

"He has been instrumental in my development as a player," says Aikman, who made the Pro Bowl each of his three seasons under Turner. "He taught me a lot and put in a system I feel I can excel in. For a guy to come in and blend all our personalities and our individual talents wasn't easy, but Norv did it."

Turner's national profile soared with the Cowboys' success. In 1994 he was the first choice of Washington owner Jack Kent Cooke to take over as head coach of the Redskins. Cooke likened Turner to former Washington head coach, Joe Gibbs, an offensive tactician with a winning background and a reputation as an outstanding teacher.

Turner, forty-three, had a painful first season in Washington. The Redskins, a team in transition, won only three games. Turner started three different quarterbacks over the sixteen-game schedule: veteran John Friesz and rookies Heath Shuler and Gus Frerotte. However, the team was competitive almost every week. Seven of the thirteen losses were by five points or fewer. Four of the games were decided in the final seconds.

Turner's history suggests he will not be down for long. He was part of winning programs at USC and the Rams before garnering his two Super Bowl rings with the Cowboys. If there is one constant in Turner's career, it is that he finds ways to win.

"Norv is one of the nicest people and one of the brightest people you ever will meet," says John Robinson, who had Turner on his staff both at USC and with the Rams. "Players will play for him because they feel like he's on their side."

Born in LeJeune, North Carolina, Turner grew up in northern

California. One of five children, Turner was raised in public housing after his father abandoned the family. Turner's mother worked two jobs until multiple sclerosis left her in a wheelchair. Norv delivered papers and worked in a furniture store to help make ends meet.

A star quarterback in high school, Turner was recruited to the University of Oregon by current 49ers head coach George Seifert, then an Oregon assistant. Turner played most of his college career as the backup to Dan Fouts, who later became a Pro Football Hall of Fame quarterback with the San Diego Chargers.

Turner spent one year, 1975, as a graduate assistant coach at Oregon before joining Robinson's staff at USC. It was there Turner met his future wife, Nancy, who at the time was employed as Robinson's secretary.

One of the great things about children is that they are totally honest. They say what's on their minds, cutting to the heart of things in a way that most adults never do.

My two oldest children, twelve-year-old Scott and ten-year-old Stephanie, did just that in 1994 when I told them we were leaving Dallas. I was giving up my job as offensive coordinator with the Cowboys to become head coach of the Washington Redskins.

The kids were stunned.

"Why would you leave the Cowboys, Dad?" Scott wanted to know.

"Yeah, why would you leave Troy and Emmitt?" Stephanie asked, referring to quarterback Troy Aikman and running back Emmitt Smith, the MVPs in our two Super Bowl victories.

Those were good questions. I'm sure there were other people, including some in the football business, who wondered the same thing.

There was no better job in the NFL than offensive coordinator in Dallas. There was so much talent on that team, it was like being paid to drive a luxury car. In the 1993 season eight of our eleven offensive starters were voted to the Pro Bowl. I could have stayed there and probably been very happy. Yes, there was a change in head coaches (Jimmy Johnson left and Barry Switzer came in), but that occurred after I made my decision to accept the offer in Washington.

I tried to explain to my children that this was a great opportunity. Very few people get the chance to be a head coach in the National Football League. When the opportunity comes along, you can't turn it down. At least, I felt I couldn't.

My situation was unusual in that I never had been a head coach at any level. I was an assistant coach in college for ten years and an assistant with two NFL teams, the Cowboys and Los Angeles Rams. I had a lot of experience and knowledge, but I'd never been the top man. Then, suddenly, Redskins owner Jack Kent Cooke was giving me that chance.

I couldn't say no.

I had two solid NFL job offers after the 1993 season; the other was to become head coach in Arizona. Though I took the Redskins job, there were plenty of people who thought I'd made a mistake, that there was more young talent in Arizona and that the team was closer to winning. I took the Washington job partly because I had such admiration for the history and tradition of the Redskins. It is a great franchise with tremendous fan support, and I'm thrilled to be part of the organization.

That might not make a lot of sense in the short term, but I was thinking long-term. I was looking for a team with stability, which the Redskins certainly have, and an area where I would enjoy raising my children.

Another factor in my decision was Mr. Cooke, the owner. He has shown over the years that he wants to win and will do whatever it takes to help his team win, whether it is paying top dollar for players or building a state-of-the-art training facility, such as the new Redskin Park. As a coach, you want that kind of owner, someone who will give you the resources to do your job.

Mr. Cooke sets high standards, so I know he suffered along with the rest of us in 1994. But we have to be realistic and accept that we're basically starting over with this team.

I knew that things were going to be rough in Washington, at least at first. The reason the head-coach job was open was that the team had not done well the year before, winning just four games. It was the Redskins' poorest season in thirty years.

The team really had slipped; a lot of the great players were at the end of their careers, and the organization needed to be rebuilt. I warned our family that we probably would not be going back to the Super Bowl for a while. Nancy and the kids understood, or at least they said they did.

The new position was a great challenge, one that really excited me. There is a scary aspect to moving from assistant coach to head coach, the same as there is in moving from middle-level management to the top of the corporate ladder. There is the uncertainty of new responsibilities, and learning how to structure your time and how to cope with the increased demands.

I discovered that there is no manual waiting on your desk to tell you what to do. You have to find a way of doing things that is comfortable and works for you. What worked for the guy who preceded you might not work for you. Everyone has his own style. You must find yours, and as I learned in my first season, it does not happen overnight.

Being a head coach is a demanding job. There are some very fine coaches, both in college football and at the professional level, who don't want to be head coaches. They are very happy being coordinators, focusing on the Xs and Os and not worrying about the other things that are part of being a head coach, such as being recognized in shopping malls and dealing with the media every day.

I've been around assistant coaches who I know would be very good head coaches. They have the knowledge and the leadership qualities, but they just don't want the responsibility and pressure, and are very open about their feelings. They have a niche and are comfortable in it.

I did not feel that way. I wanted to be a head coach. I wanted the opportunity to be my own guy, build my own team, and run it my way. I felt I would thrive on the challenge.

We had a very trying first year in Washington, finishing 3–13, but I learned a lot. I was asked a number of times if I regretted leaving Dallas. The answer always was no. I feel strongly we will put this team back on track.

My old boss, Jimmy Johnson, was 1–15 in his first season as head coach in Dallas, so where you start isn't always an indication of where you will wind up. The Cowboys went from that 1–15 to back-to-back Super Bowl victories in just five years. Something like that is heartening to remember when you have the kind of first season we had in Washington.

I was very fortunate to work for Johnson for three seasons, beginning in 1991. In effect, he made me a head coach in charge of offense. The other assistant coaches answered to me. Ultimately, of course, we all answered to Jimmy.

I created an atmosphere in which each coach was responsible for the decisions at his position — line, backfield, wide receivers, and tight ends. Those coaches worked with their players, and I spent most of my time with the quarterbacks. After practice we met as a staff, and I got the input from the other coaches about how their guys were doing.

We would discuss the upcoming opponent, what we thought we could do offensively, what we had tried before, and so on. I asked each coach for ideas but in the end, when I made up the game plan, I went with what I felt was the best package.

It was excellent preparation for being a head coach because I was doing all the things a head coach does — delegating responsibility, gathering information, finally pulling all the pieces together, and formulating a plan of attack. Of course, I was doing it for only the offense.

When I became a head coach, it was like being a coordinator three times over, that is, being responsible for all phases of the game: offense, defense, and special teams.

I found a danger — and this may reflect my inexperience as a head coach — in trying to be too involved in all areas. I may have gone a little overboard in saying, "I've gotta help with special teams," "Let me help with the defense," and so forth.

Because I'm primarily an offensive coach, I also may have bent over backward *not* to favor the offense in my decision making. We went into a few games last season short at the receiver position because I chose to carry an extra defensive lineman. Looking back, that decision probably was a mistake.

A head coach has to be aware of the entire team's needs and act accordingly; he must do what's best for the team. In business it would translate into doing what is best for the company, and not so much what is best for individual departments. You need to take the widest possible view.

The biggest single difference I found between being an assistant coach and head coach is the way time must be managed.

There are so many other things involved in the top job — organizational meetings, personnel matters, media demands — that can take you away from what you do best. In my case, my strength is offensive planning, which is what I did as a coordinator. I learned how to stay on top of my time commitments so I could give the proper attention to our offense.

Something else you have to accept when you move from a middle position to being the boss is that you have to be more authoritative. Not that you have to yell and scream like a drill sergeant, but you have to make it clear you are in charge.

I'm not a very vocal person. I've tried to keep things on an even keel with the team, but there are times when you have to stand up and say, "Okay, this is how it is, fellas."

I did it in Dallas because I took over a group of young players who had not enjoyed much success. The year before I arrived, the Cowboys finished last in the NFC in scoring. Aikman, Smith, and those guys were waiting for someone to tell them what to do on a daily basis. I gave them that direction.

This Redskins team is in very much the same situation. It has some talent but really needs direction.

Basically, I think all people are looking for leadership, are looking for direction, and want to be told how to achieve what they want to achieve. They want to be given some assurance that they can be successful. I did that in Dallas, scaling back the offense and tailoring it to the strengths of our personnel. When the players saw what we were doing, their confidence level improved 100 percent.

As a company president or a head coach, you have to provide that kind of direction. If you don't offer a plan that people can get excited about, you can't expect them to give their best effort.

I learned a great deal working under Johnson and John Robinson, two outstanding head coaches. They had very different approaches and different strengths.

Robinson, who had success both at USC and with the Rams, has great enthusiasm for the game and a real feel for people. Teams are made up of individuals, and different individuals respond to things in different ways. What motivates one person may not motivate another. Robinson is very good at finding that "M button" on each individual and pushing it at just the right moment.

Johnson is almost the opposite. He firmly believes that no one player is so important that the team cannot survive without him. He sees things less in individualistic terms. His focus is the unit. Jimmy is very demanding, but demanding of everyone equally.

One of Jimmy's strengths is his ability to make a decision, to pull the trigger. Once he sizes up a situation, he decides what to do and does it.

On the rare occasions when one of Jimmy's moves did not work out, he didn't second-guess himself. He made what he felt was the right call at the time, and he was comfortable with accepting the consequences. Many executives, in football and in business, lack that courage. They are reluctant to pull the trigger. They are afraid of the consequences, asking, "Gee, what if I'm wrong?" So they wind up doing little or nothing.

I was impressed with Jimmy's approach and used it in my first season when I made the decision to switch quarterbacks, benching Heath Shuler, our top draft pick, and starting Gus Frerotte, our last draft pick, a seventh-rounder. It was a controversial decision and didn't work out that well, because Frerotte lost three of his four starts. But I was comfortable with the move because Gus had earned the right to play, in my opinion.

I went back to Shuler, and he finished the season for us; but I did what I felt was right all along. The way our team performed as a whole, I don't think the quarterback issue mattered all that much. We had problems across the board, in every area. We have to get better; we have to upgrade our personnel. And I believe we will.

An important thing to remember is that while you may borrow ideas from the men you work under — and football coaches do it all the time — you should not try to mimic that person, no matter how successful he might be. When you finally get the chance to be the boss, stay within the framework of your own personality.

If I came to Washington as head coach trying to be Jimmy Johnson, it wouldn't work. You have to be yourself. If you try to "act" the part, the players will see right through you. I've found being straightforward and genuine is in everyone's best interest.

Beware Defensive Management

From my experience in football, I find you go through stages as a coach. There is a point when you *think* you're ready to be a head coach; then there's when you actually *are* ready to be a head coach. In some cases, those two points may be years apart. The trouble is that you never know where you are on the learning curve until you get the chance to *be* a head coach. Then you see if you really were ready, or if you only thought you were. You either sink or swim, and in the NFL there is an undertow that can pull you down in a hurry.

When John Robinson went to the Rams and when Jimmy Johnson went to the Cowboys, they had the advantage of being experienced — and proven — head coaches at the major college level. Both Robinson and Johnson had won and won big at USC and Miami, respectively. They knew how to build a program, hire a staff, and function as administrators as well as coaches.

When they stepped up to the NFL, they already had a good working knowledge of the head-coach position. They also had solid track records as winners, which gave them both confidence and credibility.

It is tougher when you make the jump as I did, becoming a head coach in the NFL without ever having been a head coach at another level. It means on-the-job training in the toughest, most competitive atmosphere imaginable. And if you mess up early, people will question your ability to do the job. This doubt can affect anyone, especially a young coach, and really can shoot holes in your confidence. The worst thing that can happen to someone who just took over a football team or a corporate office is to let a few early setbacks or criticisms rob him of initiative.

When you lose initiative, you start to second-guess yourself, back away from tough calls, and begin managing defensively. I've never been like that and never plan to fall into that trap. One of the reasons Johnson and I got along so well was we both took an aggressive approach to the game of football.

Jimmy paid me a nice compliment my first year in Dallas. He was interviewed one time and was asked about a particular play call I made. He said, "That's the way Norv plays the game, and that's how I like to play it. Be aggressive and do what you want to do."

That statement gave me great confidence as his offensive coordinator. I was not afraid to make calls that went against

the book if I felt they would work. We did a lot of that —
throwing play-action passes in short-yardage situations, for
example — and made some big plays. I knew that, whether
the play worked or not, Johnson believed in what I was doing.

As a head coach, I operate the same way. I've told my
coaches and players that. We don't have to follow the standard
NFL manual or be status quo in our approach. We will do what
we feel is best to win games. If it isn't someone else's defini-
tion of textbook football, so what? Football is a game; it's
meant to be played as a game. It should be fun, even at the
professional level. Of course, losing, like we did in 1994, takes
some of the fun away.

But my point is that I did not go into a shell or allow myself
to coach scared. That would have been a mistake. The minute
you begin thinking that way —"I'd like to call a pass here, but if
it fails I'm liable to look stupid"— you are in trouble.

You have to make decisions based on what you think is
best in a particular situation. You know your personnel. You
know the opposition. You've done your homework. If you see
the opportunity for a big play, take it. If you call something
else because it's safer and you're less likely to be second-
guessed, you are cheating yourself and your team. You have to
take some chances to win in the NFL. I coached that way in
Dallas and continue to coach that way with Washington.

Everywhere I've been, I've tried to create an atmosphere
in which there is no doubt about the fact that I know exactly
what I'm doing and that I have complete confidence in my
system. If you don't exude that confidence, you can't expect
the people around you to be comfortable with what you are
trying to get done.

Say you come in as a head coach or CEO and tell the team
or company that you are going to be aggressive, but you let the
pressure get to you and become conservative. Your players or
employees will see it immediately. They will think, "Uh-oh,
he is losing confidence." Once that feeling seeps into the team
or office, it creates all sorts of problems.

One common thread I've found in winning organizations is

that there is a system which is put in place and stays in place, so that everyone understands it and how they fit in. You need stability. You never get anywhere changing from week to week.

The Dallas offense was a good example of consistency. The Cowboys had a strong commitment to running the football, but we had a few draft picks on the offensive line who were not working out. We could have used that excuse to get away from the running game; but we didn't, because we believed in what we were doing. We just went out and got better linemen.

We made minor adjustments as we went along in Dallas, adding a few plays here and there, taking out others that we found on a percentage basis were not as successful. But the overall system remained intact.

You will find consistency in most winning organizations. The Redskins were that way under Coach Joe Gibbs. I have to put a system of my own in place now and bring in players that fit, both offensively and defensively.

One thing that happens when you move from a secondary leadership role to the top spot is that everyone waits to see how you react to things, especially setbacks. You are being tested. I certainly experienced enough of it in my first season in Washington to know.

The only way to handle it is to be organized and to have things well thought-out. That way your reactions will have a better chance of being the right ones. Most of the time, it is best to appear calm and in control. But an occasional show of temper doesn't hurt.

Jimmy Johnson was a master at sizing up a situation, whether it was a big win or a bitter loss, and giving the team just what it needed. Sometimes it was a smile and a pat on the back. Other times it was a tantrum that had players diving under their chairs.

But Jimmy made sure of two things: that everyone was on the same emotional wavelength and that everyone knew who was boss. If the man in charge can establish those things, he is well on his way to being a winner.

Perspective is a part of leadership, too. In football, as in any business, you have to accept the fact there is ebb and flow. There are times when you are winning that you feel invincible; as a coach, you think you have all the answers. There are other times when the team plays horribly and you think, "My gosh, are we really that bad?"

As head coach, you must keep everyone, starting with yourself, stable. You have to be realistic. If your team loses to a much better team, even if it loses badly, you can't panic and read things into the big picture that aren't really there.

For example, we lost twice to Dallas in 1994 by lopsided scores, 34–7 and 31–7. They were painful games to watch, especially from my position. But it did not make me question our basic approach. The Cowboys were simply a much better team. We didn't need to scrap our overall plan. We just needed to get more good, young players and to teach them how to work together.

The Dallas organization is a great model because it wasn't so long ago that the Cowboys were exactly where we are now. But they had a plan and stuck with it. With a few good drafts and free-agent signings, they built a Super Bowl team. I saw that growth firsthand. I'm trying to re-create it here.

We did not win many games in 1994 but had success in a few situations where, as coaches, we could see some promise. We'd see a play that was blocked well or a pass pattern that unfolded just right, and we'd say, "Hey, if we keep doing what we're doing and upgrade our talent so we can do it just a little better, we'll be all right."

That was the feeling I had after my first season. It wasn't much fun to lose the way we did, but I'm not discouraged. I'm looking forward to what's ahead because I know we will be much improved.

Winning Begins at Practice

As coaches, we will see to it that we are demanding on a daily basis. That is another constant in winning organizations: they know how to practice. You must practice at a high level to compete at a high level. One of the most important things I've learned in pro football is that winning does not happen just on Sunday. It happens every day of the week: in meetings, in the weight room, and on the practice field. If you can't make it happen there, you won't make it happen on game day. Winning begins with a winning work ethic, and we are instilling that in the Redskins.

Another thing I've learned as a head coach is that part of the job involves dealing with how you are perceived by the people around you. It applies in business as well. I personally think judging on outward appearances is kind of silly, but I know people work that way.

During my first preseason in Washington, I had someone say to me, "I was interested in seeing you on the sidelines in the first game. I wanted to see if you looked like a head coach, and you do."

I thanked the man but walked away wondering, "What does a head coach look like?" Tom Landry doesn't look like Chuck Noll. Joe Gibbs doesn't look like Mike Ditka. Jimmy Johnson doesn't look like Bill Walsh. And John Madden doesn't look like any of them. But they all were head coaches — and good ones, too.

My guess is you look like a head coach if you win, and don't if you lose.

If that man had seen me on the sidelines in Los Angeles when I was a receivers coach, or walking on the practice field in Dallas when I was coaching the offense, would he have said, "You know, he looks like he should be a head coach"?

I doubt it.

Some men have a presence that makes them natural leaders. I'm sure Vince Lombardi projected it when he was an assistant coach with the Giants. I'm sure Jimmy Johnson had it at every level.

But for many coaches — and I include myself in this group — it is more a matter of being in the right place at the right time. I realize that I got this opportunity in Washington because I stepped in to a great situation as an assistant coach in Dallas. As I mentioned earlier, I was surrounded by some great players and, as a coach, I made the most of it.

So when Jack Kent Cooke hired me as his head coach, I did not have any misconceptions about my "natural" leadership ability. And I was mildly amused when some articles described me as an "offensive genius."

I consider myself a good coach, but there are a lot of good coaches in the NFL. Does the fact I'm here in the position I'm in mean that I'm better or smarter than those guys? Not really. Things broke right for me, but that's how it happens in many cases. I was fortunate because I had done a good job of preparing for just this kind of opportunity. I had studied John Robinson and Jimmy Johnson to learn the basics of head coaching. Three years as a coordinator under Jimmy gave me a chance to learn to call my own shots and grow as a coach.

I stepped in to this job new, but not unprepared.

The one piece of advice I have for junior executives with designs on moving up is to prepare carefully. Learn from the people you work under. Look at situations and ask yourself, "How would I handle this if I were in charge?"

The demands of being a head coach are greater than those of being an assistant, but I've learned to keep that part of the job in perspective as well. It is very simple: I know the people to whom I'm accountable. I'm accountable to the ownership and management of the Redskins, and I'm accountable to my players. That's it. I'm not accountable to the fans, the media, the sponsors, or other outside interests.

I want to give the fans a product that is worth watching and supporting, but I will make my decisions based on what's right and wrong, not on pleasing the public or doing what some newspaper columnist wants me to do. If you get caught up in trying to please too many people, you only get yourself in a bind.

Things are different when you move up. You have to accept that fact. For example, when I was offensive coordinator in Dallas, I enjoyed having our quarterbacks come to the house for dinner. It was fun and helped Troy Aikman and me develop a very close relationship.

But now, even though I work closely with our quarterbacks, I can't have them over for dinner because if I did, I'd have to invite the linebackers another night, the defensive backs another night, and so on. As head coach, I'm the coach of the entire team. I can't favor one player or group of players over another.

I'm not saying as top man you must wall yourself off from the players or operate out of an ivory tower. Some coaches do things that way, but it isn't my nature. I want to build a feeling that says, "Hey, guys, we're all in this together."

We're a team, in other words. And I can't stress that point enough.

Another difference in being a head coach is the visibility factor. Everywhere you go, people recognize you. As an assistant coach, especially if you are fairly normal size, you can go unnoticed, and that anonymity is really nice.

One of my favorite things is going to the market and shopping for meat and produce. I've always done it, but it's hard to do when everyone knows who you are and wants to talk football. I enjoy stopping for bagels and coffee in the morning, too. But doing that was easier when I was an assistant coach and no one knew who I was. In 1994 my bagel consumption went way down.

Although I'm doing more things as head coach, I find I'm working just about the same number of hours I did as an assistant. I get to the office around 5:00 A.M. and usually work until 9:00 or 9:30 P.M.

The five o'clock habit is one I developed working with Ernie Zampese, who was the offensive coordinator with the Rams and last season succeeded me in Dallas. In Los Angeles, Ernie got to work around 5:00 A.M., so I had to get there about the same time just to keep up with him.

My body fought it for a while, but once I got into the routine, I saw the advantages. The period from 5:00 until 8:00

A.M. is a very quiet time. The phone doesn't ring; there is no one stopping by to visit. You can really focus on the job at hand.

I found it particularly good for cross-checking what we had done the day before. As coaches, we make a lot of decisions in the evening after we've looked at film. Sometimes when I come in the next morning, I look at the charts and ask myself, "What were we thinking when we came up with this?"

A little bit of distance often allows you to see things more clearly.

Despite my early hours, I don't believe in letting your job rule your life, even if it is the job you always wanted. A sixteen-hour work day may seem grueling to you, but it is fairly typical for an NFL coach.

I know my wife Nancy wishes that I did not work quite so hard, but I think it has less to do with the job than with me. I feel it is part of my nature to be conscientious. If I were a lawyer, an electrician, or a butcher, I'd probably be the same way. I don't think the long hours are unique to football coaches. We have a family friend who's a lawyer and spends every Saturday in the office. He uses the day to clean up all the loose ends from the previous week. If I were a lawyer, I'd probably do the same. I'm a perfectionist, what can I say?

But while I work hard, I still find time for my family. I try to be home in time to see the kids before they go to bed. I help Nancy tuck in the young ones. If one of them has a school play or a soccer game, I do the best I can to be there. When it is Halloween, I try to get home to help with the costumes.

Coaching is a demanding business and can really put a strain on your family. But there is an upside, too. Our kids enjoy coming to the games, visiting training camp, and meeting the players. I'm sure they will always remember celebrating our two Super Bowls in Dallas. Those are great memories.

Each coach has to find a work schedule that is right for him. Joe Gibbs, who won three Super Bowls with the Redskins, was known to sleep in his office several nights a week.

Dick Vermeil, who took Philadelphia to a Super Bowl after the 1980 season, also worked around-the-clock.

I might be a perfectionist, but I couldn't do that.

I work my hours and leave. I don't bring film home with me, either. This probably dates back to my youth — I hated homework when I was in school.

Not that my mind doesn't wander to team matters when I'm at home. I can't count the number of times my wife and I have been sitting quietly in the living room when she turns to me and says, "Okay, which play are you thinking about now? Who is the ball going to this time?"

She usually is right; football is what I'm thinking about. Like everyone else, I try to leave my job at the office — but when it is the middle of the season and the offense has not scored a touchdown in three weeks, it is tough to put work out of my mind.

Add by Subtracting

I'd like to touch on some of the things we did in Dallas because they were so successful and, in my opinion, reflect smart management.

I got a lot of credit for turning around the Cowboys' offense and for being some kind of great innovator, but that just wasn't the case. I'd like to take full credit for it, but I know better. When I got to Dallas in 1991, the offense really was struggling. The team had finished twenty-seventh in total offense in 1989 and twenty-eighth, dead last, in 1990. The latter year the Cowboys failed to score an offensive touchdown in five games and threw only twelve touchdown passes all season.

In my first year as coordinator, the team jumped to ninth in total offense and improved its scoring average by more than six points per game. A lot was written about what a creative Xs and Os guy I was, jazzing up this once-unproductive attack.

What really happened was that I came in and simplified things. I added by subtracting.

I found the old offense much too complicated. In my opinion, the players were asked to do too many things; as a result, they weren't doing any of them very well. So I stripped the thing down to basics.

I studied game films and took notes on each player, what he did well and what he did not do well. There were certain plays and formations that just did not fit our personnel. I took those plays out of the offense. Why have a play that puts *your* team at a disadvantage? It doesn't make any sense.

I trimmed the offense down to almost bare bones to pinpoint our strengths. Emmitt Smith's running ability, obviously, was one of them. Daryl Johnston's blocking from the fullback position was another. Wide receiver Michael Irvin's size and strength versus the cornerbacks trying to cover him was another. Troy Aikman's arm was a big plus, and so was his intelligence. Even as a young quarterback, he had poise and a good eye for reading a defense.

I cut the offense down by about 70 percent and retained only those plays and formations that allowed the guys to do what they could do best. At first it was extremely basic. But I wanted to make sure the players felt comfortable. I wanted an offense that was easy to grasp and one that would give the players the best chance to have some success. Once they had a taste of success and had gained a little confidence, I began expanding the offensive package, adding a wrinkle here and there. It worked out very well.

The point is — and I believe this applies to business as well — that it is much easier and smarter to start with the basics and add dimensions as you go along than it is to start with a megaplan and hope your workforce can grow into it. It is much better to allow yourself to build according to what your personnel can do rather than try to hammer square pegs into round holes day after day.

In Dallas eight of the eleven players who started on offense in Super Bowl XXVIII were with the team in 1990 when it was the worst offensive team in football. The talent obviously was there. It was the system that let them down.

As I indicated earlier, I was very lucky because what I inherited was a bunch of kids who really were ready to take off. All I did was give them an opportunity and a reason to believe in themselves. Once they had that attitude, coupled with some success, there was no stopping them.

We had a game early in the 1991 season that I thought was very important to our development. We played the New York Giants, who were the defending Super Bowl champions. We were trailing by two points with about four minutes left, and our offense was moving the ball right down the field on them.

Aikman did a great job making his reads in the face of a heavy rush. Smith made a couple of big runs on third down. Then we had the ball at the New York 18-yard line with just over a minute to go. We could have run the ball a couple of more times, kicked a field goal, and gone ahead. Instead, I called a pass play from Aikman to Irvin. We hit it for the winning touchdown.

Afterward people asked me, "How could you take a chance like that? All you needed was a field goal to take the lead. What if Aikman had thrown an interception? You would've lost the game."

Yes, that was true. But Troy didn't throw an interception, and as a result, we won more than a game. We gained tremendous confidence as an offensive unit. After that game the players realized that if they could drive the length of the field against the Giants in the fourth quarter, they could do it against anybody.

One thing about those players, and I recognized it immediately, was they had great self-esteem. Even though the Cowboys had not been successful and the offense ranked last in the league, Irvin, Aikman, Smith, and those guys still felt they could play in the NFL. All they needed was to be channeled in the right direction, which was my job.

There is a trap in coaching, and it comes from watching hours and hours of film. You see something on another team's reel — a new formation, a trick play, an unusual coverage — that catches your eye. You are intrigued, so intrigued that you think, "We ought to try that."

As a coach, you can overwhelm yourself by trying to do too much. I've seen coaches, both in the pros and at the college level, who keep adding things and changing things. They wind up losing sight of what it was they were trying to do in the first place.

I'm more of an old-fashioned thinker in this regard. I believe if you do something well and your players have confidence in it, that's usually enough. We were really a meat-and-potatoes offense in Dallas, but we won back-to-back Super Bowls because the meat and potatoes were the best you could buy.

Having been part of that organization before coming to Washington in 1994, I have a very clear picture of how much work we have to do to put this team back on its feet.

In 1994 the Redskins got off to a bad start, lost a couple of games we should have won, and never really got anything going in a positive way. I'll be the first to admit we weren't as good as we'd hoped to be. Some of our games, especially the two Dallas losses, were painful because we were so obviously outclassed.

But that's part of football, and it's part of competition. You work as hard as you can, either as a head coach or assistant or chairman of the board, and there is still no guarantee that it is going to result in any kind of a victory.

I remember the Cowboys' 1992 season. We got off to a 8–1 start and it looked like we might not lose another game. We played the Rams at home, and the Rams weren't having a very good year. We were heavy favorites, but we didn't play very well. We came out flat, which happens. But we still had a chance to pull out a win at the end.

Our offense was driving, we had third-and-five, and Aikman threw a pass underneath the coverage, which gained only three yards. We had to punt the ball away and, as a result, lost the game.

I came home that night and found my son Scott lying awake in bed. He asked me, "Why, Dad? Why on third-and-five would you throw the ball for a three-yard gain?"

All I could say was, "Sometimes things don't work out the way you plan them." A cliché, but true nonetheless.

That's the way it was with the Redskins in my first season. Things did not work out the way we planned them. But I'm not going to cry about it, nor will I question whether I made the right decision by leaving the best assistant-coach position in football to become a head coach in Washington.

All I have to do is look around at the people I've known and worked with in my years in football and consider how many of them would give anything to have this opportunity. For me to dwell on the negatives would be pretty selfish. I feel I have the best opportunity in the world and have a great deal of control over what is going to happen on this team in the coming years. I couldn't ask for any more than that.

The Power of Innovation

Bill Walsh

HEAD COACH

SAN FRANCISCO 49ERS, 1979—88

Bill Walsh is recognized as one of the premier offensive minds in football history. He spent ten years as an NFL assistant before getting a chance to be a head coach with the San Francisco 49ers in 1979.

Walsh was forty-seven when he took over the 49ers, who were coming off a 2–14 season. In just three years, Walsh guided San Francisco to Super Bowl XVI and a 26–21 victory over Cincinnati — the franchise's first NFL championship.

Walsh's teams featured a dazzling new offense, utilizing intricate pass patterns and flooding zones with receivers, bedeviling opponents with great timing, and executing plays with peerless precision. Referred to as the "West Coast offense," it is copied in some form by almost every team in the NFL today.

"Bill never had the same game plan three weeks in a row," says Ken Anderson, who played quarterback both under Walsh (when he was an assistant coach with the Bengals) and against him (in Super Bowl XVI). "He opened my eyes to the concept of ball control through the pass, proving to me that a short pass could develop into a long gain more often than a long pass could.

"One afternoon, I rolled up more than 300 yards passing and

never threw one for more than five yards. Bill was just so far ahead of everyone else in his knowledge that he seemed to reinvent the game almost every week."

Walsh built what was to become the 49ers' dynasty with a series of great drafts, which brought the team players such as quarterback Joe Montana, wide receiver Jerry Rice, safety Ronnie Lott, and running backs Roger Craig and Tom Rathman. Walsh kept the team strong through trades for budding talents such as quarterback Steve Young.

In Walsh's ten seasons as head coach, the 49ers won three NFL championships and six NFC Western Division titles. He retired after the 1988 season, which the team capped with its third Super Bowl victory. He was inducted into the Pro Football Hall of Fame in 1993.

"Bill had a great presence, great charisma," Craig says. "He would walk into the locker room and the whole atmosphere would change. He had that glow about him, the glow of a champion."

Walsh was born in Los Angeles in 1932, the son of a manual laborer. He played quarterback in high school, but switched to receiver at San Jose State, where injuries limited him to five games as a senior.

Walsh had a passion for the technical side of football. He wrote the thesis for his master's degree on "Defensing the Spread-T Offense." He worked his way up from high-school coach in Fremont, California, to college assistant, first at the University of California, then at Stanford.

Walsh's first NFL job was as an assistant with the Oakland Raiders in 1966. The following year he went to Cincinnati and its newly formed AFL franchise, where he served as offensive coordinator under the great Paul Brown for eight seasons.

Walsh got his first head-coach job at Stanford in 1977. He installed his wide-open passing game and led the team back to national prominence. In 1979 San Francisco owner Ed DeBartolo Jr. hired him to rebuild the 49ers.

Former 49ers quarterback John Brodie calls Walsh "the greatest coach ever."

"It takes three things to make a great coach," says Brodie, who played seventeen seasons in the NFL. "First, you have to totally understand the game. Next, you have to be able to organize people. Third, you have to be able to communicate to your people what you've learned and what you've organized. Bill is terrific at all three."

Walsh, who also served as general manager and team president at various times in his tenure with the 49ers, was named NFL Coach of the Year twice. After leaving the NFL, Walsh spent one year as a TV analyst and then returned to coaching for three seasons at Stanford.

He now serves as a consultant to the National Football League and conducts instructional camps for aspiring NFL quarterbacks.

M y proudest moment as a head coach was watching our San Francisco offense drive ninety-two yards to the winning touchdown in Super Bowl XXIII. It was as if all the years of practice came together in those eleven plays. It was a symphony of offensive football.

We trailed Cincinnati, 16–13, when we got the ball at our 8-yard line with three minutes and twenty seconds left in the game. Our quarterback, Joe Montana, thrived on these situations, but he never was more artful than he was in that particular game.

Under enormous pressure, with a third NFL championship on the line, our offense functioned with poise and precision. We mixed runs with short passes and threw one deep route — a 27-yard completion to Jerry Rice. The drive ended with Joe hitting John Taylor for a 10-yard touchdown with thirty-four seconds left.

That drive was a thing of beauty, the culmination of ten years of work. Each player knew his assignment and carried it out. There was no panic. The players had confidence in the plan and in each other. They almost made it look easy.

That was my last game as head coach of the 49ers. I stepped down a short time later, because the strain I was under for those ten seasons had worn me down. But winning the Super Bowl in that fashion was a gratifying way to go out. It was a defining moment for our program.

The final drive reflected what I love most about football. The artistic aspect of the game, the orchestration of the players, is beautiful to me. My strength as a head coach was in the creative process.

What we did in that drive against Cincinnati was to execute plays that I designed years ago, borrowing from various sources but creating a style that was considered revolutionary.

I've been called an innovator, and I suppose I am — in the sense that I'm naturally inquisitive and always looking for the next creative level. That creative curiosity has worked to my advantage, and I encourage anyone in coaching or business to take the same approach. Don't be afraid to try something new, even if it goes against the conventional grain. Often a new approach is the best way to go.

In the drive against Cincinnati, one reason we were successful was that we went against the so-called book. We did the opposite of what most teams do in that situation.

When most teams are driving late in the game, they throw passes to the outside, where receivers can catch the ball and step out of bounds to stop the clock. The Bengals set their defense accordingly, with most of the coverage on the outside to take away the sideline pass.

We turned that tendency to our advantage by running our patterns over the middle, where there was more room. Of course, having Montana and Rice carry out the assignments helped immensely. I don't think there ever has been a greater clutch performer at either position.

Commit to Your Ideas

Innovation is a powerful force. It can put you ahead of the competition in a hurry. It can take your team or business to championship heights. You probably will be questioned at first, perhaps even scorned. I know because I went through it.

Other coaches looked down their noses at our offense, with its emphasis on short, safe passes. They called it "nickel-and-dime" football, meaning that we were willing to play for small gains.

They were wrong, of course, as our success over the years has proven. You can control the ball as well through the air as you can on the ground, if you go about it the right way.

We proved that our style of play works — and now it seems that every team in the NFL uses what the announcers call "the 49ers' offense" or "the West Coast offense," built around the same principles. The nickels and dimes we brought to the game have become the coin of the realm. Six of my former assistants are head coaches in the NFL, and they all use that system.

You have to be committed enough to your ideas to stick it out. The worst thing you can do is kill an idea before it has a chance to develop.

I was fortunate in my years as an assistant coach to work under some men who were forward-thinking and who nurtured my creative impulses. I'm referring to Paul Brown in Cincinnati and Don Coryell in San Diego. I also worked one year with the Oakland Raiders, a team with an aggressive offensive philosophy.

When I became a head coach, I looked for assistants who were creative and open to new ideas. I urged them to look for new ways of doing things. I never wanted our team to stand still.

The style of offense that we developed with the 49ers had more dimension, more precision, and, generally speaking, better execution than our opponents'.

We pinned the offense to the timing of the forward pass much more than our contemporaries did. We perfected the timing with continual repetition. Our players would say they could run the pass patterns in their sleep. I don't doubt it.

We developed a degree of precision that allowed us to make plays in clutch situations. The timing between our quarterbacks and receivers was so precise that the receivers knew exactly when the ball would be thrown, when to turn, and where to look.

We practiced what other teams wrote off as "broken" plays — that is, plays on which the first option broke down, and the quarterback had to run out of the pocket and either carry the ball himself or find another receiver.

In fact, the most memorable play of our first championship season in San Francisco was a broken play. Montana eluded a strong rush by Dallas late in the game. While on the run, he threw a high pass that Dwight Clark pulled down in the back of the end zone to win the 1981 NFC Championship Game. Football historians now refer to the play simply as "The Catch."

To most people, it looked like a classic broken play: the quarterback scrambling away from the rush, receivers frantically trying to get open. But we worked on that play in practice. Everything was by design. Once Montana was out of the pocket, our receivers had specific routes to run, just as they would on any other play.

So on that play, Montana had several Cowboys in his face blocking his view. But he knew where Clark would be, and he threw the ball to that spot in the end zone and threw it high so that if Clark, who stands six feet five inches, could not reach it, the ball would sail out of bounds.

Some Dallas players still contend that Montana was trying to throw the ball away. They say he was as surprised as anyone when Clark made his leaping catch. That isn't true. It was a play we worked on for just that situation. It was not dumb luck; it was planning and superb execution.

One thing I tried to do was simplify the game for my quarterback. This might seem paradoxical because the perception of my offense is that it is something akin to *Star Wars,* so complex that the average athlete would have a hard time learning it. Granted, it is extensive and highly detailed, but it is drawn in such a way that makes the quarterback's job easier once he absorbs it.

In traditional offenses, the quarterback is asked to "read"

a defense — that is, to search the field for an open receiver. There is a primary receiver the quarterback looks to first. If that receiver is covered, the quarterback has to look for someone else. He has about three seconds to do all this before he is slammed to the ground by the rush.

My system made things clearer and easier. We gave the quarterback up to three options, usually to the same side of the field. He could see them at a glance and know immediately, "Option number one is not available, let's go to number two." We designed pass patterns so that someone was almost certain to be open, even if it was the running back in the flat for a short gain.

Unlike some offenses, where the quarterback stands eight yards deep and waits and waits for a play to develop, our quarterback took a shorter drop, three or four steps; made a quick read; and released the ball, often before the defense could react.

While it is labeled the "West Coast offense," I was running this same system as an assistant with the Bengals twenty years ago. Our receivers were Bruce Coslet, Bob Trumpy, and Chip Myers, all rangy athletes, working with a quarterback named Virgil Carter. It was all predicated on timing and precision.

When I went to San Francisco, our first group of receivers included Clark, Freddie Solomon, and tight end Charle Young. We won a Super Bowl with that team. When they moved on, Rice, Taylor, and Brent Jones stepped in to help us win two more Super Bowls. (It's four more, if you count the two the team has won with essentially the same personnel since I stepped down.)

In terms of talent, speed, and style, the passers and receivers I worked with on the Bengals were not the caliber of those I had on my 49ers teams. Certainly no one would compare Virgil Carter with Montana or Steve Young. Yet the offense, with its crisp timing, was productive across the board.

I still remember how it started. Paul Brown came to me and said, "We need more swish and sway," meaning more motion in the offense.

I put in more plays that started with a man in motion. That served to put more receivers in the pass pattern, which, in turn, gave us more options. It was a domino effect. Soon we had the top-ranked offense in football. And it all stemmed from the boss deciding to try something new.

I can get so passionate about the creative aspect of coaching, however, that I go overboard at times. All the people I've coached with have stories they can tell about me — and often do!

When I was an assistant at Cal, I used all three blackboards in our meeting room to diagram plays. I would start working on one play, which would trigger a thought about another play — so I would diagram that one, talking all the while. Sometimes I still would be talking about the first play while I was diagramming the next play.

Marv Levy, the head coach, followed me around with an eraser, wiping out the old plays because the other coaches would get confused.

But my mind just worked like that. I couldn't shut it off, even when I was at home. There were times when I'd be sitting with my arm around my wife, Geri, and without even realizing it, I would use my fingers to diagram plays on her back.

She knew what I was doing, of course, but she seldom said anything. Once, she waited for my fingers to stop moving and asked, "Well, Bill, did you score?" I didn't know what she was talking about, I was so lost in thought.

I couldn't help myself when I coached. I was absorbed in the game, always looking for something new. When other teams came up with a new idea, rather than simply copy it, I'd try to give it a different twist.

For example, Atlanta came up with a formation called "Big Ben," which bunched three receivers on one side of the field. It was a desperation formation, used late in games, with the three receivers going deep, and the quarterback throwing the ball their way, hoping it might be batted around and possibly caught.

I studied the play on film. While most people focused on

the three receivers, I looked to see what the defense did on the other side. In most cases, there was one receiver whom the defense would cover with just one man. Clearly, no one expected the ball to be thrown that way.

In 1987 we were trailing Cincinnati by six points with only two seconds left in the game. We used the Big Ben formation with three receivers stacked to the left, but we split Rice, our best receiver, to the other side. We hoped the Bengals would stay true to form and cover Rice one-on-one, which they did. Montana executed the play beautifully, looking to the left to hold the defense and then turning to find Rice, who beat his man to catch the winning touchdown pass.

But there is a point when an innovator can take things too far. I reached that point on occasion. I would get so excited and energized that I didn't know when to stop. Like my experiences at Cal, I would find that one idea led to another and another until, pretty soon, I was off in another world.

Usually the ideas were good ones, but we could not get them all implemented in the time we had to prepare for the next game. With the 49ers, Bobb McKittrick, our line coach, would rein me in. He would say "Bill" in a certain way, and I knew it was time to put down the chalk.

The same caution applies in business. You can have a brilliant idea, but it has to be weighed against what is practical. An innovative plan has merit only if the workforce is able to carry it out. If you are the idea man, you can't be so bullheaded that you refuse to listen to reason.

I've outsmarted myself at times. I recall a game at Stanford in 1978. We were playing USC and had a first-and-goal at the 3-yard line. We probably could have slammed the ball into the end zone with one or two off-tackle plays, but I tried to be fancy.

On first down, I called for a halfback-option pass to the tight end. I thought the play would completely fool the defense, but it didn't. The defensive back stayed right with our tight end, tipped the pass, and made the interception in the end zone. We lost by six points, and I agonized over that decision for days.

Nevertheless, football teams that are slow to move ahead get left behind. The same applies to businesses. It happened to American business as a whole because, for a time, we were trampled by the Japanese and to some extent by the Germans and others. We're coming out of it now, but we probably were guilty of not having the foresight to understand the dynamics of things. It took a major shake-up for us to be shocked into action.

I've spoken to enough corporate groups to know pro football and big business are very much alike, especially in today's workplace. Corporations operate in a very fluid atmosphere, with major changes ocurring all the time. New competition and new product lines are appearing daily, especially in the computer world. These fast-paced changes don't just involve improvements to existing products but include new concepts that can take a whole industry forward. You turn around one day, and there is someone in competition with you, beating you, that you didn't even know existed a month before.

It is like a football team that stubbornly sticks with one style of offense. Unless it changes and tries to stay a step ahead, it often will find itself losing by three touchdowns in the fourth quarter.

We are changing as a workforce, and that's good. At one time, there was an institutional approach to American business. The name of the game was production, keeping the mill running and the quotas met. Now the emphasis is on creativity, looking ahead, breaking ground.

The faster pace and tougher competition makes work at the management level extremely demanding. The stress factor is enormous. When I speak to a group of business executives, I say, "If you're losing sleep and you have a knot in your stomach, that means you're probably doing your job."

The serene four-hour workday, which allowed for a round of golf before dinner, is not as prevalent as it once was. If an executive finds himself playing a lot of golf, chances are there are people in the office doing his job and he doesn't even know it. He will come in one day to find that someone has taken over his office.

The football coach deals with the same pressure, especially if he also holds an executive position — as I did with the 49ers for several years, serving as head coach, team president, and general manager. That workload was part of the reason I wore down after ten years. I'd taken myself down to the bare metal by my final season in 1988.

Exploit the Past, Anticipate the Future

The term "innovation" implies something new, but it isn't always so. There isn't much that is truly new, especially in football. Almost everything you see today has been done in some fashion before.

That observation applies to much of our "West Coast offense." While certain elements are new, much of it can be traced to the offense Sid Gillman ran with the San Diego Chargers in the 1960s. Raiders owner Al Davis was on Gillman's staff, and he brought many of those ideas with him to Oakland. I learned about them in my one season there, 1966.

With the 49ers, we ran some plays from the Wing-T formation that Levy, now Buffalo's head coach, used at the University of California in the early 1960s. I was a coach on that Cal staff for three years. Every coach picks up ideas as he moves around.

With the Raiders, I learned the value of a fully dimensional passing game, one that forces defenses to play the whole field and thereby expose their weaknesses. Under Paul Brown, I learned how to mix power and deception in the running game. Paul had a play on which he faked a pitchout, and then ran a trap to the fullback coming inside. It was a thing of beauty.

All coaches draw from a broad base of ideas. The classic power sweep that Vince Lombardi used to devastating effect in Green Bay was part of our basic offense in San Francisco. It was a very effective weapon for us. When teams would gear up to stop our passing attack, we would hurt them with our running game.

In a 1984 NFC Divisional Playoff Game, I put an offensive guard, Guy McIntyre, in the backfield to serve as an extra blocker on short-yardage plays. For that move, I was called an innovator. The truth is, I took the idea from a former coach at Fremont (California) High School — me. I used the same formation there in 1957. (It worked then, too.)

The point is, innovation can take more than one form. It can refer to an idea that is truly new or can refer to applying an idea from the past in such a way that it seems new.

For example, you can take something off the shelf — such as the Gillman offense. You can adapt it to the current game, with its new rules and zone defenses; add a few touches of your own; and then have an offense that sets the competition on its ear. It may not be "new" in the strictest sense, but its use is innovative.

More than creating, innovation involves anticipating. It is having a broad base of knowledge on your subject and an ability to see where the game is headed. Use all your knowledge to get there first. Set the trend and make the competition counter you.

The 49ers team I took over in 1979 had won two games the previous year. We won the same number my first season. We had many weaknesses, but the most glaring was our inability to run the football.

To compensate, I used short passes instead of running plays. The off-tackle run became an off-tackle pass, and so on. Many of the principles I used were ones Gillman pioneered, such as utilizing all the eligible receivers, and putting the running backs in the patterns and isolating them on slower defenders.

While this strategy was a case of adjusting to need, it also was anticipation on my part. The NFL had changed the rules, allowing linemen to use their hands in pass blocking and giving receivers more room to run their patterns. The idea was to put more offense in the game. With our passing attack, we had a chance to be trendsetters.

In 1981, my third year as San Francisco head coach, we won Super Bowl XVI despite having a rushing attack that ranked near the bottom of the league. Our leading rusher that year was Ricky Patton, who ranked thirty-fifth in the NFL. The passing game carried us. In his first full season as the starter, Montana threw for 3,565 yards.

The next time we went to the Super Bowl, following the 1984 season, we had a balanced attack. Wendell Tyler rushed for 1,262 yards, and Roger Craig, another running back, led the team with seventy-one receptions. We used our backs in the passing game so much that Craig led the team in receptions four times in five seasons from 1984 through 1988.

Because we threw the ball so much, we were labeled a "finesse" team. I always felt that had a negative connotation. It reminded me of the "nickel-and-dime" label from my Cincinnati years.

We would defeat teams, yet they had contempt for the way we beat them. Their attitude seemed to be, "This isn't real football. Why would you play this kind of football when you could play tough, physical football?"

Their attitude toward me as a coach was similar. It was, "Who is this intruder, this interloper? Where does he get off fooling around with the pro game? His ideas won't last."

But in Cincinnati and again with the 49ers, the win-loss record usually was in our favor. Often we were winning with less talent than our opponents had. We had more dimension to our game plans, more options for the quarterback, and usually more precision in our play.

If that was "finesse" football, fine. It was successful. Instead of being just a fad, as some predicted, it became a trend.

There were some things we did that were absolutely new to pro football. We took defenses apart; nobody could understand it. Today, when I hear the descriptions of some pass patterns, I know the idea originated with me. I even can remember the first time it popped into my mind.

One specific example was a route we ran with the Bengals called "Arrow." I remember the first time we used it; it was in a game against the Steelers when they had the best defense in football. Chip Myers ran the route against Mel Blount, a great cornerback.

"Arrow" was a spin-off from another pattern that we ran all the time, a delay pattern in which we sent a running back downfield to clear a zone and brought a wide receiver underneath on a slant route. We used that play in almost every game, and good cornerbacks, such as Blount, looked for it.

With "Arrow," we used the defender's anticipation to our advantage. We ran the play against Pittsburgh the same way, with the back clearing out and the receiver, Myers, coming through on the delay. Blount recognized it and went to the inside, expecting the ball to be thrown there. Instead, Myers cut back to the outside where he was all alone to catch a touchdown pass.

Blount was totally fooled. He had taken his eyes off the receiver and was left flat-footed. It was a devastating play. We used it again later in the season against Denver and also scored a touchdown. I brought the play to San Francisco, where Clark ran it with great success. Now it is a pattern used by everyone.

Scripting plays was another idea we introduced in Cincinnati that now is used by other teams. "Scripting" means having a prepared list of plays that you intend to use at the start of each game. Years ago, coaches would have laughed if you suggested such a thing.

The idea originated, as many great ideas did, with Paul Brown. When we were together in Cincinnati, he would ask me, "What are your openers?" In other words, what do you have planned for the first series? This was our breakfast conversation the morning of a game.

Knowing that Brown would ask, I began thinking ahead and making a list of ten or twelve plays. I usually had the list completed the night before the game, so I started presenting it to our players at our Saturday night meeting. I'd say, "Here's what we're going to do tomorrow."

The players liked it. They felt it eliminated some pregame anxiety, because they knew ahead of time what they would be doing on the first series. They had a chance to think about it, and most of them said they even slept better.

From a coaching standpoint, it made sense for a couple of reasons.

First, it allowed us to make those critical decisions on our opening possession in a clinical atmosphere, with time to concentrate. You can make better decisions in that environment than you can in the heat of battle.

Second, scripting plays limited the chance of predictability. Some coaches fall into a trap in which their play-calling follows a pattern. They do not even realize it, but they find that they used the same formation on eight out of ten third-down plays. By scripting plays, you can avoid being predictable and can make a defense's job harder.

Many coaches were scornful of the idea. They would say, "How can you call a play ahead of time? You don't know the down and distance." But our script was flexible enough to allow for contingencies, such as poor field position. Yet it was hard to get some people to listen.

Those who criticized our ideas, I think, did so because they did not want to force themselves to get organized. They did not want to put the extra time into planning. They would rather wing it and hope they had some ordained vision at the moment of decision. The game would end, and they'd say, "We did the best we could." But in their hearts, they probably realized that they could have been more prepared.

Preparation Precedes Performance

I spend a great deal of time talking about preparation, because, in football and in business, preparation precedes performance. If you are better prepared than the competition, you probably will come out ahead.

But one mistake I feel some coaching staffs make — and many company staffs as well — is that while they may plan, they don't contingency plan. They put together a game plan but don't ask, "What do we do if this doesn't work?"

With the 49ers, we won a lot of games because we did plan ahead for all contingencies. So many of those crucial situations can develop — the two-minute offense, the one-minute offense, conversion of a key fourth down. We were able to handle them well because we had prepared for them.

In times of stress, you depend on your total knowledge. "Total knowledge" means knowing what could go wrong as well as what's supposed to go right. You may not want to think about the negative, but it is better to think about it ahead of time and have a plan than to be caught unaware.

Before a plan being formulated is approved, someone needs to ask, "If this starts to fail, what will we do?' " If a person has the courage to bring that possibility up, and the other people in a planning meeting are smart enough to listen, then a contingency plan can be developed. If all businesses, from football teams to large corporations, were to do that kind of planning, they would find it much easier to deal with adversity.

One thing to remember in developing a business project or a football team is that there is not going to be a perfectly smooth progression. If it were on a graph, the line of development would not be shown as a steady, upward arrow. There are bound to be some dips.

Setbacks are part of the process. There will be times of disappointment. But you still can be making progress, even though the results at the moment don't reflect it. As the leader, you cannot let the setbacks so overwhelm you that you lose sight of the overall progress.

I made that mistake in 1980, my second year with the 49ers. We had a miserable first season, but I believed we would be much better the second year. Things looked very bright when we opened with three consecutive victories. It was the first 3–0 start for a 49ers team since 1952.

There was a lot of excitement surrounding the team. We were talked about as a playoff contender, although I knew such talk was premature. We were a team in the growth stage.

From the 3–0 start, we went directly into an eight-game losing streak that marked the low point of my career. Not only did we lose eight games, but we were embarrassed by the Los Angeles Rams (48–26) and Dallas Cowboys (59–14) in consecutive weeks.

The eighth loss — to Miami, on the road — was the most disappointing, because we had a chance to win. But we killed ourselves with mistakes. In one drive, we attempted field goals twice, had both of them nullified by holding penalties, and wound up with no points.

I broke down, emotionally, on the flight home. I felt that I had failed. I was convinced I could not get the job done. I decided I would talk to our owner, Eddie DeBartolo, and offer to finish the season as coach, but that was it. I would ask for a job in the front office somewhere.

By the next day, I had changed my mind. I didn't talk to DeBartolo. I decided to wait. There was only one month left in the season. I decided to ride out the last few weeks and see what happened. As it turned out, our team won the next three games — and that success kept me going.

The next season was our breakthrough year. We had a great draft in which we acquired three defensive backs, all of whom started for us as rookies. One was Ronnie Lott. We were 13–3 in the regular season and won our first Super Bowl. That is how quickly things can change. I was ready to quit my job, convinced I had failed — when in reality, I was fourteen months away from winning the Super Bowl.

What that turnaround proved is that the line on the imaginary graph was going up the whole time. Even during our eight-game losing streak, the team was making progress. I couldn't see it. I guess I was too close to it.

Looking back, I understand how it happened.

We had taken a consistent approach and had put a lot of solid things in place in terms of our system. We just needed the horses to run with them. Once we began acquiring better players, we shot straight to the top.

It is tough when you hit that wall, emotionally. You start to question what you're doing. Some people never get through it.

In 1986 I was asked to address the American Electronics Association. That was a rough time for the electronics industry in this country. Foreign competition was threatening to put some of the companies out of business. The gentleman who introduced me said, "Bill is the only one in the room who doesn't think he should be worried about Japanese competition." The comment drew a laugh from the 600 executives who attended the dinner.

I was asked to share my thoughts on how to turn around a losing situation. Most of these CEOs viewed themselves as a losing team. They wanted to get back in the game. They just needed advice on how to do it.

I outlined my thoughts on what makes a winning organization. I talked about the 1980 season, and how I almost quit because I felt the team was going nowhere. I pointed out that sometimes the moments when you are the most frustrated are the ones when you are actually making the most progress.

I talked about creating an atmosphere of courtesy, respect, and dignity throughout an organization — from ball boys up to coaches. Creating that climate is part of building a winner.

I also talked about developing a sense of urgency, a feeling that every project on the board is vital to everyone. I stressed that as the leader, part of the job is to be visible and willing to communicate with everyone.

I've never believed in the fundamentalist approach: "Once we get point 'A' accomplished we will move on to point 'B' and when we finish 'B' we will go to 'C.' " You cannot do that in pro football, because you don't have that much time. In the NFL, by the time the team gets to "C," it probably will have a new head coach.

With the 49ers, we took a shotgun approach. We tackled a

number of challenges and dealt with them all at once. Things move too fast in this world to just poke along.

I'm a pragmatic person when it comes to coaching. I believe most games are won on preparation and execution, not on emotion and certainly not on luck. Fortune is perhaps 25 percent of the game. There are weather factors and bad calls by officials and so on. But those things usually even out over time.

I believe the emotional factor is overemphasized. Some coaches think they can win games strictly on emotion and effort. You can get away with that once in a while, but it is not something you can ride very far.

I remember being an assistant coach at Stanford and hearing the other coaches talk about how we were going to beat USC by outhitting and outhustling them. I thought, "Wait a minute. USC is going to hit and hustle, too. What are we talking about here?" You cannot pin your hopes on something as vague as effort.

But if your standards of preparation are high, there is an excellent chance your standard of play will be high. If you have practiced with discipline and poise, it will be there in the fourth quarter. *That* is how you win football games.

Be Flexible *and* Inflexible

The strategy of football has changed over the years, but so has the personal aspect of the game. I'm referring to the dynamics within the team. In my opinion, it is much harder to be a head coach today because of this factor.

As an NFL head coach now, you have a more diverse group in the locker room. You have a mix of superstars, journeyman players, and youngsters; and their expectations are totally different. You have players who want to stay, and players who want to leave.

The superstar may be the most difficult to deal with. Yet, as a head coach, you must have that person to win. You would much prefer the younger, more enthusiastic player, because he is more inclined to listen and learn. But the superstar is the one who makes the plays that win games. So you *have* to find a way to reach him.

In this unstable environment, which free agency has helped to create, the traditional role of the head coach as the leader has changed. Now the head coach is as much a facilitator as a leader. The day has passed when a head coach — or company president, for that matter — simply can bellow and expect everyone to fall in line. The leader now must be responsive to how the individual worker feels, and to what he needs to do his job. The leader has to listen as well as command.

I've always thought it important for a coach to treat his athletes as individuals, not objects. Developing interpersonal skills is critical — learning and isolating those skills, then refining them. And you must take a positive approach to teaching rather than a critical approach.

Always keep in mind that most people thrive on positive reinforcement. They can take only a certain amount of criticism, and you may lose them altogether if you criticize them in a personal way. As the head coach, you can make a point without being personal. Don't insult or belittle your people. Instead of getting more out of them, you will get less.

There are times when you may get angry and feel the need to lay down the law, but you have to do it intelligently. I sometimes staged an eruption on the practice field to make a point, but I would tell my assistant coaches about it in advance. I'd say, "I'm going to jump you today," just so they knew.

I would wait until the player I was upset with made a mistake, then I would shout at the coach, "Can't you get so-and-so to make that block?" The player got the message, but since it was not directed at him, he didn't take it personally.

There was another aspect to it. Some players would feel badly. They'd think, "Gee, I got my coach in trouble," and work twice as hard to improve.

I considered myself a players' coach, but I was not an

easygoing guy. Whenever I see a coach who is relaxed and unperturbed, I can predict with a good degree of certainty that his team is mediocre. If the man on top does not reflect a sense of urgency, the team simply will drift.

I considered myself a good motivator, although I never was one of those coaches who displayed much emotion on the sideline. There was a reason for that. I was too busy thinking.

Every moment during a game, there were decisions to make regarding what players to use, which plays to call, and how to manage the clock. As head coach, you are receiving input from all sides: from your assistants in the booth upstairs to the players who just came off the field. You have to be able to sort it all out while the battle rages around you.

There were more demonstrative coaches years ago because there were not as many decisions to make. They did not utilize personnel to the extent coaches do today. They did not have as many variables to consider. The only decision those coaches had to make was whether or not to go for it on fourth down. It's a different game now.

When I was coaching, I told people that when I appear emotionless on the sidelines, it means I'm functioning at my best. I'm into the game and not the *emotion* of the game. To think clearly, the two are best separated.

There is a dichotomy to football that poses problems for some coaches. The changing game makes it impossible to win if you are inflexible. You must find ways to adapt to the new rules, new trends, and so forth. But you cannot be flexible when it comes to the standards you set in commitment, concentration, and day-to-day work habits. Those principles must remain constant, posing one more challenge for the modern coach: how to be flexible and inflexible at the same time.

I changed as a coach over the years. One area in which I improved was my willingness to listen to my assistant coaches. I always listened, but I was a better listener later in my career. I brought out more of the creative side of my coaches, which benefited everyone.

Al Davis was good at that. John Rauch was the head coach

in Oakland in 1966, but Al was only one year removed from the job, so he still was involved in our staff meetings. He worked the room, asking questions, getting all the coaches involved, gathering information.

Paul Brown had a similar approach. As assistant coaches under Paul, we were in on everything.

Davis and Brown were strong leaders, to say the least, and both men made their own decisions. But both men saw to it that other people participated. No one was kept in the dark in either organization, and that is a smart way to operate.

You start by putting egos aside. It's the ideas that matter, not authorship. As head coach, I'd say to my assistants, "If you don't like my idea, say so."

It was open participation, but it works only if the people in the room are strong enough to tell the boss when he is wrong and then to accept the fact that their idea could be rejected as well. Just because they suggested something didn't mean it would be implemented. They had to recognize that they were involved, even if a particular idea didn't go into the game plan.

That give-and-take is the basis of open exchange. An assistant coach might go three weeks without one of his ideas being adopted. Then, on the fourth week, he may come up with the play that wins the game. Over the course of a sixteen-game season, everyone gets a chance to contribute.

To reach the championship level, the whole organization has to work together: head coach, assistant coaches, players, and management. If you have a solid foundation, it is something you can fall back on when there is trouble.

I remember the 1988 season, my last as head coach with the 49ers. We had not won a playoff game in three seasons. There was talk that the team was old and tired and, frankly, not up to the task anymore. We had quite a few injuries and had gotten off to a shaky start, winning only six of our first eleven games.

I was in my tenth season on the job and was worn down. The pressure was just brutal. As a team, we reached a make-

or-break point after the eleventh game. What I did was rely on the foundation we had built over the previous nine seasons. We had lost some games, but we had not lost that foundation.

I talked to the team in a very direct way. I said, "Here's where we are — 6–5. We still can make the playoffs. Look at our opposition. Are we as good as this team? How about that team? Can we beat that team?"

The answer in each case, the players agreed, was yes.

Then I gave the old "play 'em one at a time" speech. It refocused the whole team. We won our next four games to make the playoffs and then ran the table in the postseason, finishing up with our 20–16 victory over the Bengals in Super Bowl XXIII.

I have been asked many times to explain the team's turn-around. I've tried to explain it, but the dynamics involved is something few people outside the locker room can comprehend. There is a bonding, a pride that develops within a winning team. The players establish a standard of performance over time. The coach may not even be the one to demand it. The players will demand it of each other.

Players on great teams, such as the 49ers, are so closely knit, they won't let each other down. That is the story in military history, too. Soldiers fought for each other; that's where their courage came from. A football team is analogous to a military unit. The psychology is much the same.

The way that 1988 team regrouped and fought back, winning the Super Bowl with that brilliant 92-yard drive, was a great achievement. It demonstrated what you can accomplish with a champion's heart.

Transition Management

George Seifert

HEAD COACH

SAN FRANCISCO 49ERS, 1989—PRESENT

George Seifert quietly has climbed to the top of the NFL coaching ranks. His career winning percentage of .778 is the highest in league history, better than even that of the legendary Vince Lombardi, who is second to Seifert at .740.

Seifert grew up in the Mission District of San Francisco, rooting passionately as a boy for the team he now coaches, the 49ers. He was an usher at Kezar Stadium on the infamous day in 1957 when the 49ers blew a twenty-point lead and lost, 31–27, to Detroit in a divisional playoff game.

"It was my senior year in high school," Seifert recalls. "To see that game unfold and to remember the hush over the city following it was something I'll never forget. It was indescribable."

Seifert was named head coach of the 49ers in 1989, succeeding Bill Walsh, who resigned after leading the team to its third NFL championship. Seifert had been a defensive assistant under Walsh, devising the strategies that helped shut down Miami's Dan Marino in Super Bowl XIX and that slowed Cincinnati's no-huddle offense in Super Bowl XXIII.

As an assistant coach, Seifert was famous for his attention to detail, taking notes on index cards in color-coded ink and watching film until the wee hours of the morning.

"George is clearly the brightest mind in the game defensively," Walsh once said. "He's a dedicated football coach who possesses a great instinct for the game and great command of the technical aspects of the game."

In his first season as head coach, Seifert led the 49ers back to the Super Bowl, where they routed Denver, 55–10. He was named NFL Coach of the Year by several publications, including *Sports Illustrated, Pro Football Weekly,* and *Football Digest.*

In his first six seasons as head coach, Seifert led San Francisco to five NFC Western Division titles and two Super Bowl victories. He guided the 49ers to a 13–3 regular-season record in 1994, climaxed by a 49–26 defeat of San Diego in Super Bowl XXIX.

Seifert is a graduate of the University of Utah, where he played offensive guard and majored in zoology. He served as head coach at Westminster College and Cornell, and as an assistant under Walsh at Stanford.

The fifty-five-year-old Seifert maintained a low profile as a 49ers' assistant coach, and he still prefers to avoid the spotlight as much as possible.

Early in his tenure as 49ers head coach, Seifert came to the office one day with his hair combed straight back, making him resemble a graying Pat Riley. His new look was the lead story in the next day's local sports section. Seifert was stunned.

"I never realized things would be so different," he says, referring to the scrutiny that comes with being an NFL head coach.

Seifert's willingness to stay in the background last year prompted 49ers guard Jesse Sapolu to call him "the most underappreciated coach around."

"He knows football and he knows people," Sapolu says. "His record speaks for itself."

When I was named head coach in San Francisco, one columnist wrote that he didn't know whether to offer his congratulations or condolences.

He said I had violated the first rule of coaching: Never

follow a legend. The legend was Bill Walsh, who led the 49ers to three Super Bowl victories and six division titles in ten years as head coach.

Bill stepped down in 1989, and I was named to replace him. I had been an assistant coach with the 49ers for the previous nine years, so I knew the players and the system. I felt comfortable taking over.

But I understood why some people thought I was in a difficult spot. Bill was a tough act to follow. He set a high standard as 49ers coach, and whoever followed him would face the inevitable comparisons.

It was the same thing Steve Young faced when he succeeded Joe Montana at quarterback. No matter how well Steve played, some people would say, "Joe would've done better."

I was asked many times about the pressure of following Bill. I never dwelled on it because it was so counterproductive. I could not control what people thought of me. The only thing I could control was how the team performed, and that was where I kept my focus.

Since I inherited a championship team, I was characterized by some as a caretaker for Walsh's creation. It didn't bother me because the team kept on winning, which meant I was doing my job.

During my first season, someone said to me, "If you win, it's going to be Bill Walsh's team. And if you lose, it's going to be your team."

I said, "Then I hope it's going to be Bill Walsh's team."

I never understood that debate about whose team the 49ers are. It has been a topic of discussion in the Bay Area for years. Is it Bill Walsh's team? Is it Joe Montana's team? Is it owner Eddie DeBartolo's team? Did it become Steve Young's team in 1994?

It is very simple. The team belongs to all of us. It belongs to all those people, as well as to Dwight Clark, Jerry Rice, Ronnie Lott, Carmen Policy, and everyone else who worked so hard, on and off the field, to make the 49ers the first team to win five Super Bowls.

No one person built this organization, and no one person

sustains it. It has been, and is, a team effort. It is my job, as head coach, to maintain what already was in place. Ego has no place in the equation.

At Super Bowl XXIX, I was asked, "Is this finally George Seifert's team?" Forty-five of the players and eleven assistant coaches had joined the team since I had become head coach. There were only a few holdovers from Walsh's tenure.

I answered the question politely, but I felt like saying, "I don't give a damn whose team it is. That's not the issue. The issue is my responsibility to win games."

Maintain the Flow

We've had great success in the six years since I've been head coach. We won our division title five times; averaged more than twelve victories a season; and won two Super Bowls in impressive fashion, defeating Denver, 55–10, in Super Bowl XXIV and San Diego, 49–26, in Super Bowl XXIX.

That record is a credit to the organization, which spends the money to be the best; to the football staff, which recognizes the standard of excellence set here and works to maintain it; and to the players, who accept the challenge year after year. I'm just one part of a damn fine machine.

In taking over as head coach, I had a big advantage because I came up through the ranks. I literally grew up with the 49ers. I'm a San Francisco native and, as a teenager, was an usher at Kezar Stadium. I joined Walsh's staff in 1980 as defensive backfield coach and later became defensive coordinator.

Having been with the team so long, I understood the system. I knew how the players were treated. I knew how the team conducted itself on the practice field. As an assistant coach on three Super Bowl teams, I was part of the whole program.

I wasn't just some guy coming in from the outside who didn't know the 49ers' way of doing things — or worse, someone who felt like he had to make changes just to show he was in charge. Making arbitrary changes would have been a mistake.

The same approach applies in taking over a business. The idea of transition management is to maintain the flow. As new man in charge, especially in taking over a smooth-running operation, you would be wrong to say, "I'm going to show you how it's done." You can adjust and make small changes, as I did. But it is important to maintain continuity.

Our former center, Randy Cross, once told an interviewer, "For George to make drastic changes would be like the new CEO at McDonald's coming in and putting a McBurrito on the menu. Our current menu has worked just fine, so why alter it?"

So I didn't change many things that first season as head coach. I feared too much change would only dilute our strengths. I did a few things differently, including shortening the list of scripted plays to start each game from twenty-five to about fifteen. I felt it made our offense more flexible, but it was hardly a major change.

Another thing I did was establish that Montana was our number-one quarterback. In 1988 both Montana and Young had started, and I didn't want a situation where one quarterback was playing, but always looking over his shoulder.

I told Montana that he was our guy, and he responded with a fabulous season. He completed more than 70 percent of his passes, a career high, and threw for twenty-six touchdowns.

By trimming the pregame play script and clarifying the quarterback situation, I did not tamper with the basic framework of the team. All I did was to make the players more comfortable within the existing framework.

When I addressed the team for the first time as head coach, I stressed the responsibility we all shared. I talked about what we had accomplished the previous eight seasons, how hard we had worked to create something very special, and how it was our responsibility not to let it die. I told the players that I did not want to live off what we had done in the past. I wanted to perpetuate it, and even take it to another level.

Most of the players were veterans, so this was an appeal to

their pride. For the newcomers, it was my way of saying that just because the head coach had changed, it did not mean the standard had changed. We still aimed high. That was the 49ers' way.

One of my worst fears — something that motivates me, even today — is failure. I don't want to be the coach who lets this team go in the tank. It's a driving force within me. I use the energy created by that fear all the time.

Each organization has a different standard for success, and ours is the highest. We're expected to be in there, fighting for the title, every season. Living with that pressure can be extremely stressful, especially for a head coach. But I'm not complaining. I'd rather coach a team with high expectations than a team that has no idea what winning is.

We knew the 1989 season would be a challenge. For one thing, as defending world champions, we had history against us. No Super Bowl winner had repeated since Pittsburgh, ten years earlier. Most of the defending champions since then had either missed the playoffs or lost in the first round.

The head-coaching change also raised other questions. History showed only one previous team had won a Super Bowl with a first-year head coach, the 1970 Colts under Don McCafferty. And the last team to win back-to-back NFL championships with two different head coaches was the Chicago Bears in 1932 and 1933.

We had all those precedents facing us before we ever played a down.

Also we had a number of veterans miss the start of training camp because of contract disputes. The schedule-maker did us no favors, either, putting us on the road for the first three weeks of the regular season, including back-to-back trips to the East Coast.

We survived all that, winning five of our first six games. But then came the earthquake that shattered the Bay Area and put a halt to the Athletics-Giants World Series. Everyone's life was affected, and it was hard to expect anyone to concentrate on football after an experience like that.

Our first game after the earthquake was played in Stanford Stadium because of the damage around Candlestick Park. We played New England, and early in the game Jeff Fuller, our safety, suffered a severe neck injury that left him partially paralyzed. Jeff later recovered, but he never played football again.

It was a traumatic blow because Jeff was one of the most popular players on the team. When he was placed on the stretcher that day, less than one week after the earthquake, we all were shaken. We won the game, 37–20, but there was no joy in our locker room. As a team, we were emotionally drained.

I tried to be as positive as I could. I did not say, "Forget about it," because I knew doing that was impossible. I didn't try to hide my emotions. If anything, I let my affection for the team come to the surface.

The players knew I was giving them every inch of me, and I knew they were giving me their best effort as well. All I said was, "Guys, we'll work through this together."

And that was what we did. We took it one day at a time, one game at a time, and a close team pulled even closer together. We wound up winning fourteen games in the regular season and went into the Super Bowl with tremendous confidence. We dominated Denver, as Montana threw five touchdown passes.

I remember a Monday night game we played against the Rams. We were losing by a touchdown at halftime, and one of the coaches suggested I chew out the players when we got to the locker room.

We hadn't played well, but we were still in the game. We had an 11–2 record, best in the league. I just didn't think a tongue-lashing was in order. I gave my usual talk and made a few adjustments. We came back in the second half and won the game, 30–27.

It proves a point about motivation. Shouting at a player or a worker isn't going to make that person better unless somewhere in the shouting, there is direction. As a head coach, you do not accomplish much by yelling, "Stop 'em, defense!" It is far more effective to tell the defense, "Here's how to stop 'em." The "how-to" is what wins games. If you want to deliver it with fire and brimstone, fine. But the content is what counts.

It would be foolish for a CEO to say simply, "We need to improve production." His staff will ask, "Fine, how?" If the chief can't answer that question, he is part of the problem.

If you are up against a bigger competitor, you'd better have a strategy. If, as a head coach, I have a player who is getting his butt kicked by a superior opponent, I'd better have a strategy for him. A pep talk isn't going to do it. You need a plan that gives your player some help.

When I became head coach, much was made of the difference in style between Walsh and me. Some players were quoted as saying they were looser and happier. Montana compared it to opening a car window and getting a breath of fresh air.

I was surprised by the reaction. I think the players read more into the change than was really there. I didn't feel my approach to practice and preparation differed that much from what Walsh had done. I can be every bit as intense and focused as Bill.

The difference between us as coaches was that Walsh was more calculating. He would plan his explosions ahead of time. With me, they were spontaneous.

One day I chased linebacker Bill Romanowski off the field, cursing him, because he hit another player from behind. Another time, practice was interrupted by several scuffles, and I sent the entire team to the locker room. I have no patience for that sort of thing.

I may appear laid-back, but I have a definite flash point. Any coach or player who has been around me knows that.

The media tried to create a controversy, asking players to compare Walsh's style of coaching with mine. Some of what the players were quoted as saying about Walsh was negative, which was unfortunate, considering all he had done for the franchise.

I don't believe the quotes reflected the players' true feelings. I never asked the players about this, but I felt it was a case of where they were transferring their allegiance from one coach to another. They thought speaking negatively of Walsh was a show of respect for me. It was a way of saying, "That was the past, it's time to move on."

I steered clear of the whole issue. If others wanted to draw comparisons between Walsh and me — and I realize it was great fodder for the newspapers and talk shows — that was their right. But I had other things on my mind, like getting back to the Super Bowl.

I felt ready for the challenge. With my experience in the 49ers' system, I was comfortable from a technical standpoint. I was not intimidated by the pressure. I was prepared for that, too.

I came into the NFL as a defensive backfield coach. That is a high-pressure job because your unit is always under attack. There is nowhere on the field for a cornerback to hide, and there is nowhere for his coach to hide after a bad game. That experience was good preparation for my current role.

Working under Walsh was good preparation, too, because he was extremely demanding. He was so demanding that at times the pressure was almost excessive.

Our last few years together, when Walsh was head coach and I was his defensive coordinator, I felt that he may have deliberately turned up the pressure to harden me for the demands of head coaching. Even after a big victory, he would pick out the smallest mistake and say something such as, "That shouldn't happen." Most coaches would have let it pass, but Bill wouldn't.

Looking back, I think he was conditioning me for the job I have now.

I allowed myself to grow into the job. I did not come in with the intention of changing things right away. In time, I would make changes. But to do it the first year, just to put my "stamp" on the team, seemed ridiculous.

We are on our third offensive coordinator in seven years. Each time we bring in a new man, I tell him, "Your job is to master our system. That's what we expect to see the first year.

The second year, we might see some of you in the offense. The third year, we might see a lot more of you."

Taking over is a growth process, which means it takes time. That was how I approached being a head coach. As well as I knew our team, I needed time to grasp the big picture.

I was a head coach at the college level, but that is nothing like coaching in the pros. I was head coach at Westminster College in Utah for one season, 1965. Ten years later, I was hired at Cornell. I was head coach there for two years, and I was fired after winning three of eighteen games.

Toss in my 3–3 record at Westminster, and my career record as a college head coach is 6–21. It took me eight years after my firing at Cornell to even consider being a head coach again. I just wanted to go back to my life as an assistant coach, grow old there, and retire.

After Cornell I went to Stanford as an assistant under Walsh. When he joined the 49ers, he brought me along. Watching Bill work rekindled my desire to be a head coach. I saw how the job could be done right.

My years at Cornell, poor as they were, did teach me a lot. I learned the consequences of trying to do too much. I ran the offense and defense. I recruited. I raised money for the booster club. I even scheduled the buses for trips. I was doing all these things instead of focusing on winning games.

I also overcoached. I was so involved on the practice field, going from unit to unit and teaching technique, that I compromised the authority of my assistant coaches.

Without realizing it, I created a situation in which the players thought I did not respect my assistants. That was not the case, but that impression was what came across with my insistence on doing so much of the coaching myself. Once the players sense that kind of disregard, they begin tuning out the other coaches.

I almost fell into a similar trap with the 49ers.

When I took over for Walsh, I became more involved in the overall team. As head coach, Bill spent all of his time on offense. He didn't get involved with the defense at all. He left that to me.

When I became head coach, I had all this energy and wanted to be involved in every phase of the game. I can't say it hurt us the first season, because we won the Super Bowl. But later I reached a point in some areas where I was involved just enough to make it more difficult for the assistants.

There is a point where, as a coach, you're either going to be in it or not going to be in it. There is a saying: A little knowledge is a dangerous thing. In football a little involvement can be a dangerous thing. I realized by my third year that I was dabbling too much in the offense, so I pulled back. Things went smoother afterward.

I'd advise a businessman to do likewise. If you are promoted to an executive position, you will want to familiarize yourself with all facets of the operation, which is good. But don't get so involved that you step on the toes of the people in the field.

It's fine to ask questions and keep your finger on the pulse of things. But if you step in too often, you may rob those people of their motivation. Instead of making people more productive, which is your job, you actually may make them *less* productive.

With each year on the job, I've become better at delegating responsibility. I'm not into Xs and Os as much as I was in the past. I still enjoy that part of the game, and I think I'm good at it, but my duties as head coach have grown so much that I've done less technical coaching the past few years.

In 1994 we brought in Ray Rhodes as defensive coordinator, and I let Ray run things. Ray had been our defensive backfield coach for eleven years before he went to Green Bay as defensive coordinator in 1992. When we brought him back, he already knew our system and had two seasons as a coordinator under his belt.

Ray did a wonderful job, especially when you consider we had six new starters, including two rookies. Our rush defense improved from sixteenth in the league in 1993 to second in

1994. We also tied for the NFL lead with twenty-three pass interceptions.

Ray did such a good job that after we won Super Bowl XXIX, the Philadelphia Eagles hired him as head coach. To replace Ray, we brought in Pete Carroll, who had been the head coach of the New York Jets. I have given Carroll the same wide latitude I gave Rhodes.

Present Ideas, Not Mandates

With the advent of free agency and the salary cap, the head coach fills more of an administrative role than ever before. The business is so fluid, with personnel decisions being made every day — and each of those decisions is tied to dollars — that it takes up a tremendous amount of time. You must compete as aggressively in this area as you do in the games, or you will be left behind.

Our front office did a great job in 1994 when we signed a dozen free agents, including Pro Bowl players such as cornerback Deion Sanders, linebackers Ken Norton and Rickey Jackson, and center Bart Oates. Each signing was a complicated process, requiring hours of meetings and discussions, but it paid off for our team in a fifth NFL championship.

I find myself coaching differently now — and it is due, in large part, to free agency. With so many players changing teams each year, it is essential that a head coach be flexible. You have to adjust to your personnel.

A perfect example is the 1994 season when we signed Sanders. It was mid-September, we were into the regular season, and we had a defensive scheme that we had practiced all summer. Adding Sanders changed the whole picture.

Deion is the best one-on-one pass defender in the game. It would have been foolish to have signed him and stayed with the same game plan we had before. Sanders brought unique skills to our defense, so our coaches had to move things around to take full advantage of his talent.

We changed our coverages to allow Sanders to play man-to-man on his side of the field. That allowed us to play more double coverage on the other side. It also allowed us to move Merton Hanks from cornerback to free safety, where he blossomed into a Pro Bowl player.

The result was a vastly improved defense that helped us win the Super Bowl. It happened because our coaches were flexible enough to redesign our defense on the fly.

My main responsibility as head coach is to create an environment in which it is possible for my coaches and players to succeed. You don't achieve that atmosphere by being a dictator. Look for the best way to get things done. Let your coaches coach, and play to the strengths of your athletes.

I present ideas, not mandates. If something works, we go with it. If it doesn't, we try something else. What worked one year may not work the next, so you must be willing to find another way.

If you can't learn, or aren't willing to try, you can't coach in this league.

The demands of this job are tremendous. The pressure is unrelenting, especially with this team because of its high visibility and the expectations of the fans and management. It began with Walsh in the 1980s, and it was part of what I inherited with the job.

I generally can cope with it, but there are times when it builds and builds until it is almost overwhelming. There were occasions, even in our Super Bowl seasons, when I wished I could be Forrest Gump.

In the film, Forrest Gump took off running and ran for three years. I wanted to do that. I wanted to just start running; maybe in three years they would find me in some desert, and I'd still be running.

That was how I felt at one point in the 1994 season and in 1992, when we had to make the decision about what to do with Montana. We wound up trading him and were vilified for it.

This is an exhilarating business, yet it can be punishing

emotionally. For example, I went through the whole range of emotions in 1994. It was a season that ended with our team winning the Super Bowl, but it was very trying at times. I had the Forrest Gump urge more than once.

The season began with the media speculating that I might be replaced as head coach if the team did not win the Super Bowl. We had lost to Dallas in the NFC Championship Game each of the previous two seasons, and a lot of people — both inside and outside the organization — were frustrated.

Team president Carmen Policy did a masterful job of managing the salary cap so we could sign the best group of free agents in the league. We rebuilt the defense, which had been our weak link the previous year. Getting past Dallas and winning the Super Bowl wasn't just a goal for our team, it was a mission.

Adding to the pressure was the fact most preseason forecasters had picked us to win the NFL championship, partly because of the changes in Dallas after Jimmy Johnson stepped down as head coach.

In July a Bay Area newspaper ran a headline that read, "Bye, George." The message was that if our team fell short again in 1994, I would be out as head coach. I did my best to ignore the issue, but it exploded after an embarrassing 40–8 loss to the Eagles in the fifth week.

That game proved to be a rallying point for our team on the way to the Super Bowl, something I'll discuss more later. But at the time, it really heated up the debate over my future.

A local radio station asked its listeners, "Who would you rather have coaching the 49ers, Jimmy Johnson or George Seifert?" The result of the phone-in poll: 85 percent wanted Jimmy Johnson.

Asked for my reaction, I said, "I'd like to thank the fifteen percent who voted for me." I tried to make light of it, but I was really hurt. Hurt and surprised.

If you had told me ahead of time how the poll would turn out, I would have laughed at you. I was the local guy. I grew up in San Francisco, for Pete's sake. I was a part of the four

Super Bowl championship teams. I would have thought that counted for something.

I was embarrassed by the poll, embarrassed by the whole furor. It was one of those situations where your ears are red because you know people are talking about you.

I felt the scrutiny, but it was pointless to stew about it. I took my anger over the whole issue and used it as motivation. I surprised myself with how passionate I became. I reached a point where I said, "The hell with it. I'm going to get this thing done."

I did not ask DeBartolo or Policy where things stood. At that point, what were they going to say? Even if they gave me a public vote of confidence, what did that mean? I had to win, that's all. I had to finish the job we started at training camp.

Three months later, after we had defeated Dallas in the NFC Championship Game and had beaten San Diego in Super Bowl XXIX, it was an unbelievable feeling. I know this sounds dramatic, but I felt like a sea captain. The waves were splashing over the sides, the rain was blowing in my face, but I still brought the ship in. I weathered the storm. I've done it twice now, my first season as head coach and again in 1994.

Winning is the intoxicating part of this business. The fact that you can be so far down at one point in the season and then standing on the crest when it's over takes your breath away.

One of the things I inherited when I took over the 49ers was an aging nucleus of veterans. Montana was thirty-three; Lott was thirty; Roger Craig was almost thirty and wearing down. These players were regarded as treasures in the San Francisco community and rightly so, but the time was coming when they would have to be replaced.

That job fell in my lap. I knew the day I became head coach that it was part of my responsibility. Cutting them wasn't something I looked forward to, because I knew much of the success I had enjoyed as a coach was due to the efforts of those players.

I loved those guys and respected them; but as the head coach, I had to look to the future. We had to start bringing in younger people. I knew it was not going to make me popular. Yet if I couldn't face up to that responsibility, I shouldn't be the head coach.

We tried to make the transition as smoothly as possible. Lott and Craig left as free agents after the 1990 season. In the college draft that year, we acquired Hanks and running back Ricky Watters, talented youngsters who helped lead us back to the Super Bowl in 1994.

The situation with Montana went on through 1992. By then, Joe was thirty-six. He had missed the entire 1991 season and virtually all of the 1992 season because of surgery to repair a torn tendon in his right elbow. Young stepped in and led the NFL in passing both years.

We let Montana play in the final 1992 regular-season game against Detroit. He played very well — completing fifteen passes, including two for touchdowns — and proved that he still could do the job. Montana did not want to be a backup. He wanted to be the number-one guy again, and many 49ers fans wanted him back in that role with our team.

We had to make a decision.

Young had played extremely well. In fact, he was the NFL Player of the Year in 1992. It did not seem reasonable either to trade Young or to bench him. I still believed Montana could play, but I questioned whether he could hold up physically for an entire season.

To bring both quarterbacks to camp the following season risked dividing the team, so we traded Montana to Kansas City. We were criticized for trading a legend, but it was the best thing for all parties. Joe got a chance to be a starter again, and he took the Chiefs to the AFC Championship Game. Young continued to improve. He led the league in passing a record four consecutive years [1991–94] and was named MVP of Super Bowl XXIX.

It irritated me that for so long there were people in the Bay Area who seemed determined to create something negative out of having two players the caliber of Montana and Young.

There was this "Joe versus Steve" feud, which the media helped fuel and had the fans taking sides.

I think the area was damn lucky to have both of them. We had the greatest quarterback of all time in Montana. Now we have Young, who has played phenomenally well. Like Joe, he is on his way to the Pro Football Hall of Fame.

What a great thing for the community to have both of these players here at the same time. That is why it ticks me off when I see a headline like the one that ran after our victory in the 1994 NFC Championship Game. It said: "Joe Who?"

It was meant to flatter Young and make the point that he had escaped Montana's shadow. But to me, it almost cheapened what Steve had done.

Joe Montana is a part of what we're fighting to maintain here. What Steve is doing now, crazy as it sounds, is for Joe, too. It is like what I'm doing now is for Bill Walsh, too. We're trying to keep the whole thing going.

It gets back to the issue of "Whose team is it?" It is part of us all. The coaches and players today are carrying the torch for the ones who put this team in motion.

Let the Horses Run

There has been a great deal of turnover on this team, much more than with the Pittsburgh teams of the 1970s, for example. The Steelers won four Super Bowls with essentially the same coaches and players. If you look at our five NFL championship teams, the cast changed dramatically from year to year. Yet there was the same drive and sense of purpose.

For this consistency, I credit great leadership, much of which came from the players themselves. They establish the work ethic. The coach can say, "Let's have a good practice." But it is the players who ensure that it happens by setting a high standard for each other.

There are times as head coach when the best thing I can do

is move out of the way. My ego isn't so large that I have a problem with that.

In each of our last two Super Bowl seasons, there were times when the team chemistry was so strong I almost felt shoved in the corner. At moments like that — and they're fleeting — I have to reaffirm what I believe my responsibility to be.

My responsibility is to win games and win championships. And if that means every now and then feeling shoved aside, there is nothing wrong with that. I can't overreact. If I do, I risk disrupting a good thing.

So I ride it out. When there is a need for me to step forward again, I do.

I was especially sensitive to the team chemistry aspect in my first season as head coach because, as part of transition management, I felt the best thing I could do was maintain the championship flow of the previous year.

We had a veteran team with five players, including Montana and Lott, who had been on the three previous Super Bowl winners. It was a team driven by the desire to do what few teams had done: that is, win Super Bowls back-to-back. Those players really took it upon themselves to get it done that year.

The 1994 team was different.

Whereas the 1989 team was fresh off a Super Bowl victory, most of the players on the 1994 team never had been to a Super Bowl. Twenty-four of the players were new to our team, reflecting the impact of free agency.

The 1989 team was an older group, with the workmanlike attitude you would expect from veterans accustomed to winning. Our 1994 team was younger and friskier, with a cockiness that, for me at least, took some getting used to.

In the past the 49ers were known for being rather low-key. We did not go in for a lot of flamboyant behavior, such as trash-talking and end-zone dances. We maintained what I call a corporate image. We took care of business in a clean and professional way. That was Walsh's style and it was mine, too.

But these are the 1990s and, as I'm constantly reminded,

the athletes have changed. They like to talk; they like to strut and show emotion. Our 1994 team certainly reflected that.

Watters brought some of that style to our team in 1991, but it really took hold in 1994 when we signed Sanders and drafted William Floyd, a fullback from Florida State. They were players who believed in having fun; talking up a storm; and, when they got the chance, dancing in the end zone.

Their attitude proved infectious, and soon more players on the team were doing these things. Even Rice, the consummate craftsman, was laughing and having a good time. Even the most conservative coaches, including me, responded in a positive way.

It was obvious enough that the press picked up on it. During the network telecasts, the announcers talked at length about "the new 49ers."

As head coach, I had a choice. Do I put a stop to it and insist that we go back to being the corporate 49ers? Or do I let this new personality evolve and see where it leads?

I took the second approach, although I made it clear to the players that I would step in if things went too far.

As it turned out, I did not have to say very much. I spoke to Floyd a couple times about things he did on the field, gestures that I felt crossed the line of good sportsmanship. He listened. Otherwise, there were no problems.

At Super Bowl XXIX Young said, "I really want to give George credit for what he has done this year. He let the reins go and let the horses run."

It was an interesting analogy because that was exactly how I saw it. That team was like a great stallion, and I had to give it the reins and let it go. I honestly felt that if I tried to impose too much of myself on that team and be too restrictive, the whole thing would have crumbled.

It was a refreshing year in that respect. It was fun to be around those players every day. There were so many characters in the locker room. That was one of the things that kept me going when the pressure really mounted.

The thing I've enjoyed most about coaching pro football is

the mix of personalities. In college the players are alike in age and often come from the same area. But it is not that way in the pros. It is a true melting pot. There aren't many places in the world where you can find such diversity and see it work together so well.

Young, Rice, Sanders, Jackson — all great guys, all different. Coaching is most enjoyable when you get a group such as the one we had in 1994, where the players can have fun and still not lose their focus.

If our team demonstrated anything in the 1994 season, it was that players can wear bandannas, spike the ball, dance in the end zone, and even taunt the other team — but still can focus on football.

I maintain there is a line — call it good sportsmanship, good taste, whatever — that should not be crossed. I also believe the players and coaches have a responsibility to the organization to respect that line. But you still can do that and high-step a little, especially if you do it as well as Sanders.

Our 1994 team was the hungriest team I've ever been around, because our veterans had their noses rubbed in the mud the previous two years by the Cowboys. They were embarrassed and angry. We also added several free agents, such as Sanders, Jackson, and linebacker Gary Plummer, who had won all sorts of individual honors but never a Super Bowl.

The team had a burning desire to get past Dallas and win the NFL championship. It was particularly acute for Jackson, who was thirty-six, and Plummer, who was thirty-four. Both thought this was their last chance for a Super Bowl ring. Young was extremely focused as well, because he wanted to prove he could take a team all the way, as Montana had done so often.

Yet for all that emotion and hunger, our team was slow to put things together. It may have been all the new faces; it may have been the scheduling. We opened with a Monday night game against the Raiders; Rice scored three touchdowns to surpass Jim Brown as the NFL's all-time touchdown leader with a total of 127. We went directly from Los Angeles to a game in Kansas City against the Chiefs and Montana. We lost that one, 24–17.

Those were two highly charged, emotional games to start the season. We probably were a little drained as a result. We won our next two games over the Rams and Saints, but things were not clicking. We all felt it — the coaches, the players, everyone — going into the Philadelphia game.

Part of it was the pressure, especially after the signing of Sanders, where all we heard was, "You guys have all this talent, you'll win the Super Bowl easily."

If you hear that day after day, the pressure builds and builds.

Another problem was a lack of continuity on defense. We had six new starters on that side of the ball, including all three linebackers. There were five free agents in the group, all from different teams. Rhodes had his hands full getting them to play as a unit.

They did not believe in what we were doing, defensively. Each player was questioning the other player. Each guy had his own way of doing things, and no one wanted to work together. One guy was playing the Phoenix defense, the next guy was doing what he did in New Orleans, and so on down the line.

I talked to the team about it. I remember saying, "Something is going to happen with this team. I don't know if it will be a big win, a big loss, or a fight between a coach and a player or what. But something is going to happen, and it will pull this team together."

I felt something like that coming. It was building and exploded with the loss to Philadelphia. The Eagles scored the first two times they had the ball; led, 30–8; at halftime; and wound up handing us our worst loss ever at Candlestick Park.

We were missing four starters on the offensive line, and the Eagles defense was knocking the daylights out of Young. In the fourth quarter Young was flattened on two consecutive plays, and I decided enough was enough. I sent our backup quarterback, Elvis Grbac, into the game.

Young was steaming as he came to the bench. He was furious that I would lift him in the middle of a series. He felt that by pulling him and leaving the other ten players on the field, I was singling him out as the culprit.

That wasn't the case at all. I simply wanted to spare him further punishment. I did not want to risk him for even one more play. We could not afford to lose Young; and the way things were going, that was what was likely to happen.

When Young came to the bench, he stalked around and shouted several profanities in my direction. I kept my attention on the field, but I was aware of what was going on. Our quarterback coach, Gary Kubiak, did his best to calm Young down.

I understood his frustration — we all felt it — and it carried over into the next game against Detroit. We fell behind, 14–0. For a time it looked like a replay of the Philadelphia game. Steve was getting killed on every play, but still he was battling his heart out.

Finally Steve got knocked down and couldn't even get back on his feet. He literally crawled off the field on his hands and knees. The players on the sidelines went berserk. They couldn't take any more. They had to either face up to the challenge right then or roll over and die.

That was the moment I had talked about, the one that would pull all these individuals together and make them a team. We rallied to score four touchdowns and won the game, 27–21.

The Philadelphia and Detroit games blew all the carbon out of our engine. Things smoothed out after that. The next week we went to Atlanta and beat the Falcons, 42–3. We put together a ten-game winning steak; our team scored thirty-five or more points in seven of those games.

It was a great streak, and we all knew where it was leading: back to another showdown with Dallas in the NFC Championship Game. This was what we had worked all year to achieve. This was why we brought in the free agents to rebuild the defense. This was going to be The Game.

After all I went through that season, with the speculation

about my job security, then the radio poll, I probably should have been nervous as hell going into the playoff game against Dallas. But I wasn't. On the contrary, I was on fire.

I never was more excited about a game. I never had such a burning desire to get something done. It was so out of character for me that my wife and children didn't know what to make of it.

My wife said, "Gee, this is fun. Usually we're all sitting around, biting our nails because you're so nervous. But you're having so much fun this week, we're all excited."

That was truly how I felt. There was such finality to that game; so much was riding on it that it was almost a high. It was like the excitement of putting a million dollars on the line and rolling the dice. There was a charge that was unlike anything else I've ever felt in football.

The thing was, I was totally confident about the outcome. I knew we were going to kick their butts. There was no doubt in my mind. It didn't matter that they were the defending two-time world champions. We were going to take them apart. I could sense it.

All week, walking through the locker room, my body became electric with the feeling. We had gone through so much to put the team together, and there was so much frustration built up from having lost the previous two years. There was no way we were going to lose that game.

When we did win and were presented with the George Halas NFC Championship Trophy on the platform on the field, with all our fans watching and cheering, it was the greatest feeling. I wouldn't have traded places with anyone in the world.

Staying the Best

Chuck Noll

HEAD COACH

PITTSBURGH STEELERS, 1969—91

Chuck Noll coached the Pittsburgh Steelers for twenty-three years before he retired in 1991. He won 209 games, the fifth-highest total in NFL history, and is the only NFL head coach ever to win four Super Bowls.

A private man who cared little for the spotlight, Noll transformed the Steelers from the NFL's most downtrodden franchise into a dynasty. Prior to Noll's arrival, the Steelers never had won a division title. Under Noll, they won nine AFC Central titles and posted fifteen winning seasons.

Bob Smizik of the *Pittsburgh Press* wrote: "There has never been a stronger force in sports in Pittsburgh than Chuck Noll. . . . He stands alone for his accomplishments, for his style, for remaking a franchise."

Few people had heard of Noll when he was hired by Steelers owner Art Rooney Sr. in 1969. At the time, Noll was a thirty-seven-year-old assistant coach with Baltimore, shaking off the disappointment of losing Super Bowl III to the underdog New York Jets.

Noll's first season in Pittsburgh was a painful one as the Steelers went 1–13. But he rebuilt the team with a series of great drafts that brought in players such as Joe Greene, Terry Bradshaw,

Franco Harris, Mel Blount, Jack Ham, Lynn Swann, and Jack Lambert. The Steelers won their first division title in 1972; then became a playoff fixture for the next decade.

Noll displayed little emotion on the field and seldom berated his players. If he was angry, he simply stared. That was enough. "Being on the wrong end of a Chuck Noll glare was all the motivation you needed," guard Chuck Wolfley once said.

Born in Cleveland, Noll attended the University of Dayton. He was a twenty-first-round draft pick of the Cleveland Browns in 1953. He played seven years for head coach Paul Brown as an offensive guard who helped shuttle in the play calls from Brown to the quarterback.

"Chuck could have called the plays without any help from me, that's the kind of football student he was," Brown once said.

Noll attended law school and sold insurance during his career, but when he retired as a player in 1959, he chose to stay in the game as a coach. He spent six years as a defensive backfield coach with the San Diego Chargers before he joined Don Shula's staff in Baltimore.

When Noll took the head-coach job in Pittsburgh, his friends tried to talk him out of it. Says Noll, "They told me I was crawling into a graveyard of coaches. I didn't believe it. Any team can win if it does things right."

Under Noll, the Steelers did things right for almost a quarter of a century. They won with a dominating defense, nicknamed the "Steel Curtain," and a balanced offense led by Bradshaw, Harris, and the acrobatic Swann.

Six of his Steelers are enshrined in the Pro Football Hall of Fame. Noll himself was voted into the Hall of Fame in 1993, his first year of eligibility following his retirement.

"Of all the people who were involved in the Steelers' organization during our Super Bowl years, Chuck is by far the most deserving of induction into the Hall of Fame," says Ham, Pittsburgh's stellar outside linebacker and fellow Hall of Fame enshrinee.

Many football coaches are one-dimensional figures with few

interests outside the game. Noll is a Renaissance man. He is a licensed pilot, a gourmet cook, a wine connoisseur, an accomplished scuba diver, and a patron of the Pittsburgh Symphony.

While he often gives terse answers to football questions, Noll enjoys talking at length about things such as the Juilliard String Quartet and photosynthesis on the ocean floor. Noll still lives in Pittsburgh, where he donates his free time as a volunteer with the blind.

O ne question I'm asked constantly is, "Which is harder, taking a team to the top or staying at the top?" I was fortunate enough to do both as head coach of the Pittsburgh Steelers.

But I wish I had a better answer to the question. I tell people both tasks are equally difficult. At least, that was how I felt when I was in the middle of it, helping to build a championship team in Pittsburgh in the 1970s and keeping it focused enough to win four Super Bowls in six years.

Being the best and staying the best are different challenges. I never felt one was easier or tougher than the other. Each involved winning, and there is nothing easy about winning in the National Football League. The second phase — that is, maintaining a level of excellence — is of great interest to me. But I can't discuss it without describing how we built our first Super Bowl team, because that was the foundation for what came later.

When I was hired by the Steelers in 1969, the team had not won as much as a division title. In thirty-six years of operation, the franchise had had only eight winning seasons — and one of those was 1943, when it merged with the Philadelphia Eagles for one year [because of wartime manpower shortages] and finished 5–4–1. All the years of losing had given the Steelers and the city an inferiority complex. There was a feeling of resignation, that the Steelers never would turn it around. It was summed up in the letters "SOS," which in Pittsburgh stood for "same old Steelers."

In my first season as head coach, we won our opener against Detroit, 16–13; then lost the rest of our games to finish 1–13. I heard a lot of "Yeah, new coach, but it's SOS."

So what I faced was a battle not only for the minds of the players but also for the minds of the fans. I had to turn the attitude from negative to positive before we could accomplish anything. That is no small task, and it doesn't happen overnight.

Conversely, once we had some success and had won our first back-to-back Super Bowls in 1975–76, the challenge became keeping things in perspective. As a coach, you constantly preach the need for maintaining the same approach to work and preparation, win or lose. My former coach in Cleveland, the great Paul Brown, had a saying: "There is only one way to coast and that's downhill."

We had some great teams in Cleveland. One reason the Browns stayed at or near the top every year was Paul's ability to maintain his own focus and to be sure the players did the same.

I tried to emulate that focus with our team in Pittsburgh. I told our players that winning a Super Bowl was like walking a tightrope. If you look down and see how high you are, you may get dizzy and fall. But if you keep your eyes straight ahead and focus on the next game, you will keep going.

One reason we had such success with the Steelers was we had a group of players who believed in that approach. They understood there was no such thing as "arriving." They never let up and, once they were on the tightrope, never looked down. They kept going forward.

The first few seasons, when we were putting things together with the Steelers, were really the basis for our achievements later. We did not look for a quick fix. We were not interested in just patching holes so we could win three games in a season instead of just one.

I felt confident enough in my relationship with the team owner, the late Art Rooney Sr., and his son Dan, who then was vice-president, that I could take time and build the right way, with players who had the ability and attitude to win a championship. Each year added more players who fit that description. Once we had the pieces in place, they stayed in place.

Twenty players, almost half the roster, played in all four of our Super Bowls. The reason we were able to stay on top as long as we did was that we picked the right people to begin with. They were the kind of people who not only could win but also could endure.

Being a winner is a day-to-day thing: teaching, learning, and growing. A team must grow together, and it does not grow immediately; it takes patience.

This method applies in business as well. When you start, you present your program, teach it, see how it works, and then make your judgments based on how everything fits.

Those judgments must concern players, coaches, personnel people — everyone down the line who is involved in helping to make the team a winner. It works the same way in business. Look at all the departments; then let the workers know where they fit in.

As head coach, I wanted each department to think it was the best, had the best people, and served the most important function. If workers get the impression that they don't matter, they are likely to perform that way.

Aspire to Be the Best

As I stated earlier, our goal at the start in Pittsburgh was not respectability, although there were some people in Pittsburgh who would have settled for that after the Steelers averaged fewer than four victories in the five seasons prior to my arrival.

My goal, which I set as the team goal, was winning a championship. In my opinion, that is the only thing worth setting as a goal. You cannot be the best without first *aspiring* to be the best.

If you make a .500 record your goal, that's likely all you ever will achieve. If you make ten wins in a season your goal, you are sending a message that that is good enough — and it simply can't be, not if you ever hope to win a Super Bowl.

One of the problems I found when I took over the Steelers was that the majority of players had been down so long, they had forgotten what it meant to be a winner. They were interested in one thing: hanging on to their jobs. Their goal was to be on an NFL team, but not necessarily the best NFL team. As a coach, you won't go far with those players. I weeded them out as quickly as possible.

I inherited a few good players — five of whom were part of our first Super Bowl team — and we added more in our drafts. Still, it was a long haul from 1–13 our first year to 5–9 the second year and 6–8 the next. It took time and patience to see the thing through.

In the early years, other teams tried to take the few good players we had. They would offer a package of three or four of their backups for one of our better players. The other general managers would say, "These players might not start for us, but they could start for you."

My response was simple: "No, thanks."

If you build a team with other people's backups, what are you really building? How can you expect to beat these teams if you are playing with guys who weren't good enough to start for them?

Some teams that are down a long time make that mistake. They settle for the incremental gain: "These players aren't great, but they're better than what we have now" is their thinking. Coaches simplify their offensive and defensive approach so they can increase their victory total by one or two games.

That misses the big picture. If you want to build a top-flight team or corporation, you set the highest goal as your standard and make all your judgments accordingly. You put in the offensive and defensive philosophies that you feel will win a championship, and you assemble a group of players who fit your plan. Stick with what you believe in even though it may take a little longer to attain. The end result is worth it.

Build on Attitude

When I came to Pittsburgh, I sat down with Art Rooney Jr., the club's personnel director. I told him the kind of team I wanted to build and what kinds of players I wanted to build with. I wanted good athletes. More than that, I wanted good athletes with good attitudes. I wanted players who were talented, but also motivated and mature.

There are many impediments to winning, and most of them lie in the area of attitude. Nothing impedes problem solving more than a lousy attitude, and attitudes are like a virus — they're contagious. A bad one can spread through a locker room in a hurry.

But a good attitude can be passed around as well. That's what I was looking for — a nucleus of players with the ability to win and an attitude to match.

On every team, there is a core group that sets the tone for everyone else. If the tone is positive, you have half the battle won. If it is negative, you are beaten before you ever walk on the field.

I told Art Jr. that we should build through the draft as much as possible, select players from winning college programs. I wanted players who knew how to win and wanted to win. That was the quickest way I could think of to rid the team of the "SOS" syndrome.

If you look at our first Super Bowl team, we had wide receiver Lynn Swann and guard Gerry Mullins from USC, linebacker Jack Ham and fullback Franco Harris from Penn State, quarterback Terry Hanratty from Notre Dame, and other players with similar solid football backgrounds.

They were young guys — winners — and a welcome breath of fresh air for the franchise.

Something I noticed when I took over the team was that all the leadership was verbal. Guys talked about making plays, talked about winning, but it did not translate into action. I wanted players who led by what they did, not by what they said.

That was why we selected defensive tackle Joe Greene with our first pick in the 1969 NFL college draft. Greene was a relatively unknown player from a small school, North Texas State. When we selected him, the reaction among the Pittsburgh fans was "These guys don't know what they're doing." One newspaper headline read: "Joe Who?"

But we had studied Greene closely and felt he was ideally suited for what we were hoping to build. He had size (six feet four inches, 275 pounds); speed; and what scouts call "a great motor," which means he played hard all the time. He was a leader by example.

When Joe arrived at our first training camp, he changed the face of Steelers football. He was so good and so relentless, even in practice, that he set a tempo which made the other players work harder. He became the measuring stick of what we wanted in a football player.

We got defensive end L. C. Greenwood, a future all-pro, in the same draft. The next year, we drafted quarterback Terry Bradshaw and cornerback Mel Blount, both future Hall of Famers. Each year we added a few more pieces and soon had a Super Bowl contender.

Another plus was moving in to a new facility, Three Rivers Stadium, in 1970. That move underscored the point we were trying to make, that it was a new era for the Steelers, one committed to winning.

Previously the team had practiced in a public park. The locker room was located in the basement of an old hospital. The team played its home games at Pitt Stadium on the University of Pittsburgh campus, which meant the Steelers really didn't have a place to call their own.

At the new stadium, there was a carpeted locker room and spacious meeting rooms. We practiced and played our games in the same facility. It was a morale boost, especially for the veteran players who often had complained about the conditions at South Park.

Dan Rooney made a statement at the time that rang true. He said, "Now we're going first class. Before, the Steelers were transients."

As we were putting things together, we developed a motto, "Whatever it takes."

"Whatever it takes to win," I told the team, "that's what we will do." As our team grew, we built on that philosophy.

Essentially, we were talking about teamwork, winning as a team, which is misunderstood by many people. I've heard teamwork referred to as a fifty-fifty proposition, everyone sharing the load equally.

Well, teamwork is never fifty-fifty. It never was and never will be.

Any team or business that thinks it can operate that way is wrong. Fifty-fifty may sound good in theory, but it isn't practical. If you wait to see what someone else on your team or in your company is doing so that you can match it — which is the whole idea of fifty-fifty — guess what? By the time you figure it out, the game is over and you've lost.

Real teamwork, winning teamwork, has nothing to do with things being divided equally. More accurately, it's everyone working together to get the job done, which isn't the same thing. If one part of the team isn't holding up its end, then everyone else has to pick up the slack.

That was how we came up with "whatever it takes." That was how we defined teamwork, and as a principle, I feel it applies across the board.

If your business is going to succeed, everyone in the operation should understand that concept. If one division of a company is off, the other divisions have to crank it up. A year later, perhaps the roles will be reversed. The point is that everyone understands they're in it together with a common purpose.

The best example of this concept in action that I can recall was our team during the 1972 season, when we were trying to clinch our first AFC Central Division title. It was the next-to-last week of the regular season, and we led Cleveland by one game. We could not afford to stumble — or we risked losing what we worked so hard for all year.

We went to Houston to play the Oilers, and our offense was in terrible shape. All the linemen were down with the flu. Hanratty was out with an injury; then Bradshaw dislocated a finger on his passing hand in the first quarter. We had to use a rookie quarterback, Joe Gilliam, and couldn't move the ball at all.

We had problems on the defensive side as well. Greenwood was out with an injury and our other end, Dwight White, was playing hurt. If we had gone by the fifty-fifty concept of teamwork, Joe Greene could have packed up his stuff and gone home at halftime because he had done more than his share to keep the game close for thirty minutes.

But Joe was the ultimate "whatever it takes" player. Knowing that the offense couldn't score and that the defense was weakened, Joe took it upon himself to win the game. He moved from tackle to end to fill in for Greenwood and played one of the greatest halves of football I've ever seen.

We never did score a touchdown, but we did bleed out three field goals to take a 9–3 lead. The Oilers had the ball in the final two minutes, still with a chance to win, but Greene sacked quarterback Dan Pastorini on three of the last four plays to preserve our lead.

The next week we defeated San Diego, 24–2, to win the first division title in franchise history. It was a great moment, but it was made possible because Greene had carried the team on his back the previous week in Houston.

In our last two Super Bowls, 1979 and 1980, the situation was the opposite. Our defense did not play well, but the offense, led by Bradshaw, carried the load as we defeated Dallas, 35–31, in Super Bowl XIII and the Los Angeles Rams, 31–19, in Super Bowl XIV.

None of these games broke down fifty-fifty, offense and defense, yet they were textbook examples of teamwork. Guys picked up for each other and made the plays necessary to win. I didn't have to spell it out for them. They knew what had to be done, and they did it.

I can't point to one thing and say, "This is why we were able to sustain our success." It involved a number of factors. We not only won four Super Bowls in six years, but we also went to the AFC playoffs ten times in thirteen years, which is a pretty good run.

How did we do it?

I go back to the way we assembled our team. We didn't draft strictly for talent and certainly didn't draft for marquee value (remember "Joe Who?"). Rather, we drafted players we felt had the attitude and character that fit our program. We wanted players who would last, who would give us something to build on.

In the six NFL drafts from 1969 through 1974, we selected sixteen players who took part in all four of our Super Bowl victories. Six of them are in the Pro Football Hall of Fame, and I'm confident that others, such as Swann and center Mike Webster, will soon follow.

With that kind of foundation — so many great players all in their prime and growing together in the Steelers' system — we were able to build a team that stayed on top longer than most.

Credit our scouting department for finding most of the players. A few we lucked into, such as safety Mike Wagner, an eleventh-round draft pick in 1971 who developed into a ten-year starter.

We drafted Webster in the fifth round, and he wound up playing fifteen seasons with us, a club record. Webster was listed at six feet two inches and 250 pounds, but he was barely six feet tall. Most NFL scouts say you can't play center at that size. Other teams passed on him for that reason, but we loved his toughness and his competitive drive. He proved to be a great player and leader for us.

Looking back, I feel we were lucky to have our run when we did because it was easier then. There weren't as many outside influences. There wasn't the player movement they have in the NFL today with free agency and a salary cap. There weren't as many third parties involved, such as agents and other people pressuring players to write books and so forth.

There weren't a lot of people chasing our guys, especially after the first two Super Bowls, because we took everyone by surprise. We got more attention the last two championship years. By then most of the players were older and knew how to handle it.

Today I hear so many coaches coming off great seasons talking about distractions and jealousies within the team caused by salary disputes and such things. I feel fortunate because we had very little of that kind of problem, at least in part because it was a different game, on and off the field, in the 1970s.

Consistency, Not Complacency

As head coach, I didn't do very much differently from one year to the next. One thing I learned — and I learned it early — was not to single out a player for blame in public.

I once made the mistake of saying Blount had missed an assignment on a key play. It was written up in the papers, and the fans booed Mel the rest of the season. I made sure I never did that again.

When I felt the need to criticize a player, as often as possible I tried to do it in private. I didn't want it in the newspapers and didn't like doing it in front of the other players. I tried to keep that stuff, and anything else negative, behind closed doors.

One of the things we did as a coaching staff was evaluate the team each season. It was almost like starting over every year in the sense that we looked at each player, each position, and said, "Okay, where do we stand? Are we good enough or do we need to upgrade?"

In doing this evaluation, especially after Super Bowl years, we paid particular attention to attitude. Were the players still hungry? Were they as focused as they were the year before?

One thing I stressed in speaking to the team was that nothing would bring us down quicker than complacency. I included myself in that warning. In the NFL no one's job is secure. If you don't produce, you don't last. It doesn't matter what you accomplished in the past.

We had signs posted around the camp, slogans such as "One Is Not Enough" and "Two Is Not Enough." After our fourth Super Bowl victory, the slogan was "One for the Thumb," meaning let's win a fifth championship ring. We never did get that one, but the signs were there as a daily reminder.

Some people may think this is corny, especially when you are dealing with professional athletes, men in their twenties and thirties. But I think it can be very effective. The signs are there to remind the players of two things: the job at hand and the hard work involved in earlier wins.

I did not believe in having a lot of rules, but we did have some — and the players were expected to obey them. And the rules were the same for everyone; that uniformity is the only way to have harmony. The rules weren't for punishment and weren't for the money we collected in fines. They were to keep everyone on the same page.

I've heard about teams on which there are different sets of rules — one for the superstars and another, stricter, set for the other players. That does more harm than good. It drives a wedge between players who have to work together on the field.

One time Joe Greene went out for a pizza and missed our curfew by five minutes. I could have looked the other way or said, "Next time you do that, Joe, it will cost you." But it wouldn't have been fair to the players who abided by the curfew every night.

Instead, I said, "That pizza will cost you fifty dollars, Joe."

He paid the fine without protest.

I would have done the same thing if it had been Bradshaw, Swann, or Franco Harris. We were very consistent in the way we dealt with our players; that fairness was another reason we were successful over a long period of time. We did not have a lot of cliques and jealousies in the locker room.

In any business, consistency is important. If one group of workers feels another group is getting special privileges, whether it is longer lunch breaks or better parking spaces, it's bound to cause friction that will interfere with production. As the person on top, you make the rules — so you'd better apply them fairly and wisely.

Not only didn't we have a lot of rules but I didn't have a dress code. For example, on road trips players could wear whatever they wanted. I felt they were grown men and could make their own decisions. I told them only one thing, "Remember, you're representing the Pittsburgh Steelers, so dress for success."

It was quite a fashion show in the 1970s. Bradshaw wore jeans and cowboy boots. Greenwood carried a shoulder bag, which earned him the nickname "Hollywood Bags." Halfback Frenchy Fuqua drew the most attention. He liked to wear platform shoes with plastic heels that he filled with water and goldfish selected to match the rest of his outfit.

The writers, who knew me as a conservative guy, asked what I thought of Frenchy's attire. I'm sure they thought I was seething but, really, I wasn't.

I said it was fine. Frenchy liked it. The other players got a kick out of it. So what was the harm?

As both a player and a coach, I always believed that you did not have to sacrifice your individuality to be a part of a team. You had to be willing to work together with everyone else, but it didn't mean you had to look and dress like everyone else. Just because a bunch of guys wear team blazers on the road doesn't mean they think or play like a team.

Likewise, I did not attempt to censor what our players said to the media. I didn't threaten them with fines if they said something inflammatory. I said they were responsible for their own words. If they said something dumb, they had to deal with the consequences. It wasn't junior high school.

The bottom line is that if you do a good job picking your people, as we did in the 1970s, you don't need a bunch of rules, because the people are able to handle things. Also it helps if you have quality leaders on your team to keep everyone in line.

We had some excellent leaders, particularly Greene and Jack Lambert, our middle linebacker. Like Greene, Lambert was a leader almost from the first day he arrived at training camp in 1974.

Most rookies defer to the veterans. Lambert was not that way. He had such great natural intensity that he never thought in terms of who was a rookie and who was a veteran. He only thought about one thing: winning.

We had a lot of focused individuals on our championship teams, but Lambert was the most demonstrative. He did not tolerate any fooling around, even in practice. If someone made a silly mistake or cracked a joke in the huddle, Lambert jumped right in his face.

As a coach, I loved having a player like that.

Lambert was a classic overachiever. He was six feet four inches and 215 pounds, which was light for a middle linebacker. But he was such a fierce competitor that he became the best player at his position in the entire league. He was voted into the Pro Football Hall of Fame in 1990.

There's a lot to be said for that kind of leadership within the ranks. That is the Japanese concept of management: not a dictatorship where one man at the top says, "This is how it's going to be," but a system in which all parties at all levels work together.

That was how we operated in Pittsburgh. As head coach, I relied a great deal on my assistant coaches; as a staff, we relied on the leaders within the ball club to keep things together. Everyone shared in the responsibility — so when we won, everyone shared in the team's success.

Interestingly, one of my most satisfying years in coaching was 1989 when we finished 9–7 and advanced to the second round of the playoffs. We had a very young squad that was written off by most people early in the season. In terms of talent, that team certainly did not compare with our Super Bowl teams. In 1989 we had twelve rookies on the roster and twenty-nine players with less than three years of NFL experience. It was a very raw team, but it was a team that worked hard to get better every week.

We opened that season with two humiliating losses, 51–0 to Cleveland and 41–10 to Cincinnati. There was a lot of criticism directed at the team and me after those games. It would have been easy to explode or panic, but I'd been around long enough to know that getting upset wouldn't have accomplished anything.

I told the team, "What we're doing will work. We just have to work harder and do it better."

We kept plugging away, won a few games, gained confidence, and wound up getting into the playoffs. We did not win the Super Bowl — we didn't even make it that far — but I still was very proud of that team because I knew it gave me all it had to give.

One of the worst things you can do, either as a coach or corporate head, is take an idea and try to jam it down the throats of your staff or players. Ideas, even good ones, have to be sold to the team first, then objectively evaluated on the field.

In football — and this distinction applies in business as well — there is the "what to do" and the "how to do it." The first part is the plan, what you have on paper or in your head. The second part is the application: how your idea actually works on the field.

Some people would say the first part is the most important because without a plan, you have nothing. I think the second part is more important because that is where your team gets its confidence. A plan isn't worth a thing if the team isn't sold on its merits.

This is where, as a coach or boss, you have to put your ego aside. In football there is no pride of authorship. Only one thing matters: getting the job done. So if you come up with an idea that you think is brilliant, but when you put it on the field, the players cannot grasp it or they don't have the speed or whatever to make it work, the worst thing you can do is say, "I don't care. This is my idea and we're going to make it work."

Well, it won't work, and it also will cost you respect in the eyes of your coaches and players.

Good management involves give-and-take. Your job as head coach is to give the team its best chance to win through preparation. That means coming up with a game plan the players can believe in, not one that creates doubt.

We did well as a football team because as coaches, we eliminated — or at least minimized — doubt. As a result, our guys played with a lot of confidence and aggressiveness: they believed in the plan and believed in each other. They believed they were going to win, regardless of the opposition.

When players have a fear of failure, it's hard to overcome. It restricts an athlete and can stifle him as an individual. If he continually worries about failing, he will get so damned tight that he *will* fail. It is critical that, as a coach, you do everything possible to wipe that fear away.

I tried to do that when we went to our four Super Bowls, especially the first one in January 1975. There is so much hype involved in the Super Bowl that it can unsettle and distract a football team.

I had been through one Super Bowl before, as an assistant coach with Baltimore in Super Bowl III. It wasn't the most pleasant experience, as we lost to the New York Jets, 16–7, in a game that some people said was the biggest upset in pro football history. I know the hype upset *us*.

We had had a great season in Baltimore in 1968, winning thirteen games and losing only one. We dominated Cleveland, 34–0, in the NFL Championship Game. The press built us up as one of the great teams of all time. All the acclaim may have blinded us a bit going into the Super Bowl, especially because no one thought much of the Jets and the American Football League at that time.

Then we played the game, and Jets quarterback Joe Namath taught us all a lesson. That game left a lasting impression on me, and I tried to use that experience in preparing the Steelers for Super Bowl IX.

I warned our players to maintain their perspective. I knew the press would gush about our Steel Curtain defense. I told the players to take all the flattery with a grain of salt. I reminded the squad that no matter what was said in the press, we still had to go out and play the game. We had to go on the field and prove we deserved to be world champions. It all came down to that. Everything else was prologue.

I also did my best to lighten the atmosphere. Too many teams get to the Super Bowl and let the event overwhelm them. They worry about spending a week on the road, living in a hotel, and practicing in unfamiliar surroundings — all the peripheral stuff.

That sort of mentality is counterproductive and usually comes down from the top. If the head coach harps on the interruptions in the training schedule and the daily media obligations, the players will pick up on it. Pretty soon they'll be thinking more about the peripheral stuff than the game.

I took the opposite approach. I told the players to enjoy themselves. I feel the Super Bowl should be a celebration, a culmination of a great season. I wanted the guys to have fun. You work all season to get there, why make it a burden?

We played well in our Super Bowls because the players were loose. Most of them enjoyed the interview sessions, which took place each morning at the hotel. With other Super Bowl teams, I heard about players who dreaded meeting the press. Some players did not go to the interview room at all and were fined by the league.

For the most part, our players were just the opposite, especially the first year. Our team had been down so long, the players were grateful for the attention.

In Super Bowl IX, at the end of the first media day when the press buses were loading, our center, Ray Mansfield, chased after the reporters, shouting, "Come back. I'm not done yet!"

It reflected the attitude of our team. We took things in stride.

The first question I heard every day was "What about the pressure?" This was particularly true before our first Super Bowl because our opponent, the Vikings, had been to two previous Super Bowls, and it was believed that an experienced team had a huge advantage over a team that was appearing in its first title game.

I didn't buy that theory, and neither did our players.

The Super Bowl was a football game, and we had played twenty-two of them that season, counting the preseason. It wasn't a new thing, but everyone in the media wanted to make it more than it was.

So, really, I didn't think experience was a factor; when it came time to play, the better team would win. I feel that approach served us well.

By the time we went back for our last Super Bowl [XIV in 1980], the questions had changed. I was asked, "Is this scene old hat for your team now?"

The answer, of course, was no.

It was the same game, the same stakes. And the motivation was the same — to be the best. We wanted to win just as much, so we worked just as hard.

I was proud of the way our teams performed in the Super Bowl. We played dominating defense against Minnesota in Super Bowl IX, allowing only seventeen yards rushing, a Super Bowl record. We defeated Dallas in both Super Bowls X and XIII, each time by four points. We came from behind in the fourth quarter to beat the Rams in Super Bowl XIV, 31–19.

None of these victories came easily. Our teams demonstrated great poise. That composure was characteristic of those ball clubs. It goes back to the "whatever it takes" philosophy.

Much was written about the Steelers, and our defense in particular, intimidating the opposition. It wasn't something we designed or tried to do. It happened because our teams played hard and played with great focus, which came from within the athletes themselves. I never saw the need to apologize for it, although there were some negative references to our "image" as if it were this sinister thing. When I was asked about it, I would say, "I can't be responsible for what you think of me. If I intimidate you, that's your problem."

That irritated some people, but I think it is true.

One thing that arose from our style of play — and this is the price of success, I suppose — is the league passed rules that were aimed directly at reducing our effectiveness. Our defense was dominating teams to such an extent, it seemed to me the NFL decided it had to do something to give our opponents a chance.

A rule was passed forbidding a defensive back to make contact with a receiver five yards beyond the line of scrimmage. That neutralized a technique we used, called the bump-and-run, in which our cornerbacks used their size and strength to push receivers around and disrupt their pass patterns.

Another rule loosened the restraints against holding. Under the new rule, offensive linemen were allowed to extend their arms and use their hands to ward off defensive players. That gave blockers a much better chance to tie up our pass rushers, who had fifty-two quarterback sacks in fourteen games in 1974.

If you get way out front, you can count on somebody changing the rules at some point. That change is something you must be prepared to deal with if you are very successful, either in sports or in business. When it happens, you cannot mope and say, "That's not fair." You have to come up with a solution.

We began mixing our coverages, not relying so much on the bump-and-run, although Blount was such a great defender, he made it to the Hall of Fame anyway. And while the blocking rules made it tougher, Greene still was more than most teams could handle.

If you are good enough, you'll find a way. But count on it getting tougher every year. You have to be smart enough and flexible enough to adjust.

Play to Win *Every* Game

As head coach, my role was twofold during those Super Bowl years. I was a builder, helping to gather the material and assemble the team. I also was as a fine-tuner, keeping the thing humming along. I didn't meddle for the sake of meddling. If things were going well, I might not say a word. I didn't have to.

I did not give many pep talks. As a motivational device, I think pep talks are overrated anyway. In football you win games with good preparation and good execution. If you have those two elements, speeches aren't necessary.

I knew I didn't have to say anything before the really big games, such as the four Super Bowls. The players knew what was on the line and knew the price they paid to get there, so by game time they were ready to go. On those days my pregame talks consisted of just a few words and no rah-rah.

I talked more on the days when we played lesser teams, when I thought the players might not be as focused. If I sensed that the team was flat, or if we had not practiced very well, I might be a little more forceful in my pregame remarks.

Recently it was called to my attention that our team in the 1970s had an amazing record against the so-called weaker teams in the league. In an eight-year span beginning in 1972, our team won fifty-nine of sixty games played against teams with a losing record.

I wasn't aware of that statistic until someone pointed it out. I felt it was a tribute to our team that it played hard every week and was not prone to letdowns. It would have been possible for us to drop a few of those so-called easy games because everyone was gunning for us. A losing team could make its whole season with a win against the Super Bowl champions.

There is a huge responsibility that goes with being a coach or the top man in any business. It's not for everybody. I didn't grow up dreaming of being a coach — it just sort of happened for me. But I'm glad it did because I can't imagine anything that would have given me greater satisfaction.

I thought about other careers, even as I played football for the Browns. I went to law school at night while I was playing and realized very quickly that practicing law was not for me.

What I disliked about law was the very thing I liked about football, which is that law is built on confrontation, while football is built on teamwork and bringing people together.

The other career I considered was insurance. I worked in that field, too, and took all the sales-training courses. I liked it well enough, but not well enough to stay in it. It was good training for coaching, however, because it taught me how to deal with people.

In sales training we were taught never to take "no" as a flat answer. If a customer said no, you asked, "Why not?" You tried to find out why that person said no. Once you heard his objections, you had something to work with. You could see if there was a way to change his mind.

Sometimes it didn't work. Sometimes "no" meant "no." But other times, you could turn "no" into a sale by asking the right questions and coming up with the right answers.

Selling is part of coaching because you have to be able to sell your program to the team. You have to deal with any objections from assistant coaches or players. You must ask questions, identify the problem areas, and see what can be done to bridge any gaps. You must do these things before you can do anything else.

This is where you can see a real correlation between football and business, between coaching and management. They are very much alike. I once made the statement that the only difference between football and life is that in football, you have a scoreboard.

Actually, the statement wasn't original. It was first suggested to me by a CEO at a conference where I spoke about building a winning organization. He said, "You're lucky. You've got a scoreboard."

It was the first time I had thought of it that way, and he was right. We are lucky in football because we do have a scoreboard. I can look up in the third quarter to see if we're ahead or behind and by how much. In business or in government, you often cannot tell where you stand until it's too late.

The successful coaches, especially in pro football, have the skills to be successful executives in almost any field. I really believe that. I had the advantage of playing for, and coaching under, some of the best. I learned things I was able to apply when I got my chance as a head coach in Pittsburgh.

As I indicated earlier, I played for Paul Brown in Cleveland, and I was an assistant coach under both Sid Gillman in San Diego and Don Shula in Baltimore. The first two men already are in the Pro Football Hall of Fame; Shula is sure to be inducted after he retires.

From Brown I learned the value of basics, that the game really is won by the team that blocks and tackles the best. Shula, like me, played for Paul, so he reflected the same philosophy. Don would say, "We don't want to fool them, we want to beat them." It was just another way of saying "Stick to basics."

The thing I remember about Gillman was his unquenchable curiosity. He was much more the deep thinker. He loved to dissect films of other teams to see what they were doing, to determine if it was a step ahead of what we were doing.

I learned from each of these men. However, when I was given the chance to be a head coach, I did not attempt to copy them. To me, a copy is nothing more than a second-rate imitation. I had my own approach, which was somewhere in between Gillman, Brown, and Shula. I also felt I kept learning every year I was on the job, so my approach to the game changed and developed.

I was characterized as unemotional and cold. Almost every profile written about me included words such as "aloof" and "dispassionate." One columnist wrote: "A divine seer could've stared into Noll's eyes for a week and walked away scratching his head."

There is a big difference between perception and reality — what appears to be and what really is. I may have appeared unemotional because I did not vent much on the field, but I was emotionally involved. Trust me on that.

No one can be involved in the game of football and be without emotion. It's impossible. The game itself is emotional. Just because someone does not display much emotion doesn't mean the emotion is not there. Every time we took the field, I had emotion welled up inside me, but I seldom let it show.

I felt emotion could get in the way of decision making during a game. You only have so many seconds between plays to decide what to do. If you use up twenty seconds stamping your feet and screaming at the officials, you've wasted valuable time. I hate wasting time.

I also kept a low profile during my years as a coach. Early on I got a reputation as a bad interview because I preferred not to talk about myself. People would come in to write about "the real" Chuck Noll — that sort of thing. They did not get very far because I preferred being private.

I understood we were in a public business and there was a certain amount of visibility that went with it, but I kept it within bounds as much as possible. I did not talk about my inner thoughts, in part because I did not want to give the people I was competing against any kind of feel for my mindset. I felt that if I remained a mystery, it was to my competitive advantage.

On another level I didn't want to compete with my players for media attention. The same was true of endorsements. I did one endorsement — it was for a Pittsburgh bank — as a favor to a friend. Other than that, when I got an offer, I said, "Give it to one of the players."

I felt that as head coach, my primary focus should be football, not selling snow tires or car batteries. Also I recognized that players are only in the game for a short time. I wanted them to reap as many of the fringe benefits as possible while they could. I didn't need the money and didn't care about the exposure.

I did not have a TV show or radio show for the same reasons. I know most NFL coaches have those shows, but I did not want to do them. Dealing with the media questions on the job was quite enough exposure for me. To repeat the process on radio and TV seemed to me redundant.

For years I kept a plaque on my desk with a quote from Pope John XXIII: "See everything. Overlook a great deal. Improve a little."

In many ways, that was my approach to coaching: Be aware of what is going on around you. Overlook the things that don't matter. Work toward getting better every day.

We all could learn from that.

Current and former NFL head coaches are available for speaking engagements. For further information, contact David Houghton, NFL Properties, Inc., at (212) 838-0660.